Consecrate Every Day

SUNY Series in Modern Jewish History
Paula E. Hyman and Deborah Dash Moore, Editors

Consecrate Every Day

The Public Lives of Jewish American Women
1880–1980

JUNE SOCHEN

State University of New York Press ● *Albany*

To Ruth Sochen, Joyce S. Schrager, and Phyllis Neiman

Published by
State University of New York Press, Albany

© 1981 State University of New York

Printed in the United States of America

For information, address State University of New York Press, State University Plaza, Albany, N.Y., 12246

Library of Congress Cataloging in Publication Data

Sochen, June, 1937–
    Consecrate every day.

    Bibliography: p.
    Includes index.
        1. Women, Jewish—United States—Biography.
2. Jews in the United States—Biography.
I. Title.
DS115.2.S6   920'.0092924073 [B] 80–29169
ISBN 0–87395–526–9
ISBN 0–87395–527–7 (pbk.)

Contents

Preface

In 1976, the Women's Division of the Jewish Federation of Metropolitan Chicago asked me to speak on the role of Jewish women in American history. It seemed to be an appropriate request. I am an historian of American women who is Jewish. However, there was one serious problem. I was not a specialist on the lives of Jewish women in America. But the subject intrigued me; it appeared to be a natural synthesis of my interests in women and in the group of women of which I am a part. I accepted the invitation and proceeded to investigate the sources available on the subject. I soon discovered that the material, especially secondary-source information, was sparse. Male historians of Jewish America paid little or no attention to women. My experience in researching women's history, of course, should have prepared me for that fact.

I had to decide how to pursue the topic. During the course of my research (the speech became the beginning and not the end of my efforts), a few books were published on Jewish American women. They have been a helpful introduction but did not deal with the themes and issues that came to interest me. While *Consecrate Every Day* used both primary and secondary sources, its contribution, I believe, is in its presentation of broad categories of the public experiences of Jewish American women: the focus upon volunteer activists, factory workers, writers, and professionals. I am particularly interested in those Jewish American women who publicly discussed the role that Judaism played in their lives.

As in most human endeavors, many people participated in the making of this book. Friends and colleagues discussed the subject with me, read the manuscript at various stages, and offered constructive criticisms of it. Professor Lawrence Fuchs of Brandeis University was an early and helpful reader; Professor Melvin Urofsky of Virginia Commonwealth University was a later and helpful reader. I thank both of them for their penetrating and important comments. The three anonymous readers for the State University of New York Press also deserve acknowledgement as I found their questions and concerns very useful. This book is dedicated to my mother, my sister, and my friend, three Jewish American women who are living examples of the harmonic synthesis of Judaism and modern American life. Ultimately, I am solely responsible for the interpretations and viewpoints expressed in these pages.

June Sochen
Northeastern Illinois University

1. Introduction

Jewish women, as Jewish American women, have experienced both unanticipated pleasures in the new American environment and the expected responsibilities of the Judaic tradition. They have continued to be the homebodies, the keepers of tradition, the mainstay of family ritual. As in modern Europe, they worked outside of the home as seamstresses, salesclerks, and professionals. But America also provided a new experience, a previously unknown dimension to their lives. It gave Jewish women the opportunity to go to school for longer periods than ever before, to study "secular" subjects, to learn new occupations, and to assert their individual rights. Jewish women in America became discrete people, individuals regarded with respect, interest, and sometimes hostility in the individualistic culture of America.

The novelty of the American experience for Jewish women was not immediately evident, nor were its possibilities quickly realized. That is the twentieth-century story for Jewish American women, a story of struggles and of successes. Jewish American women were garment workers in the emerging factories of urban America and participated in the early efforts at unionization. They also appeared in the ranks of middle- and upper-class women active in a variety of philanthropic, religious, and cultural organizations. Jewish American women became social reformers and social workers, volunteers and professionals in twentieth-century America. In so doing, they mirrored the diversities and tensions in both the Jewish and American cultures. They worked to create new equations that included both elements.

Jewish American women distinguished themselves in various public activities because of the ambivalent richness of their dual background. It was precisely their remaining rooted in the Judaic culture while living in the secular American world that gave them the fresh perspective, the agonizing need to redefine themselves, and the impetus to move outside predictable forms. They articulated, and acted out, the desire to realize their individual human potential, an American and Jewish ideal, within a Jewish and American secular community that held very rigid views about the roles of women.

Jewish women expressed the dilemmas of being a woman with ambition and intellect in a society that viewed all women in traditional ways. They have been leading social critics of both Jewish and American society; they have written of the tragedies and joys, of the tugs-of-war between competing but equally important needs—of family, self, society, and tradition. They invented organizations, stories, and other means to harmonize their ideals with life's unpleasant realities.

While immigrant Jewish mothers often resisted the individualistic temptations of the new country, their younger sisters, daughters, and granddaughters seized the opportunity to gain recognition and rewards on their merits for themselves alone. Ambitious Jewish women in the 1910's found the business world inviting but also discovered that living too fully in the secular Christian world endangered their links with their Jewish roots. Preserving the ties to Judaism, rejecting them, or working out a series of accommodations became the basic strategies employed by Jewish women in their quest for self-fulfillment and social acceptance. The hopes and dreams of America did not always mesh with the hopes and dreams of their Jewish parents.

Immigrant mothers in the early twentieth-century prided themselves on saving enough money for their sons to go to City College; their daughters secretly saved to go to Hunter College, the women's teacher's college of New York City. Perhaps unknowingly, immigrant mothers led the way toward their daughters' emancipation. They gave up wearing the customary *shatel*, the wig that symbolized their traditional commitment to female modesty, and they allowed, however reluctantly, their teenage daughters to imitate the fashions and makeup of their native American counterparts. Early-twentieth-century American commentators spoke of the "new woman" and the increased number of job opportunities available to her. Jewish women became avid attenders of lectures and Americanization classes. They applied the Jewish reverence for learning (heretofore reserved for men only) to the seemingly infinite opportunities of American public education, beginning a long process of self-definition and accomplishment.

Contrary to the popular view of Jewish American women as being narrowly focused upon family, home, and hearth—indeed, jealously guarding the home against outside invasion—Jewish American women have had rich public lives throughout the century. They were among the first Americans who identified the social problems that needed solving in urban-industrial America; they raised money, attended meetings, and lectured on the merits of their cause with zeal and patience. Their life experiences demonstrate a continued commitment to society and to a large social vision. As industrial workers, volunteers in social-service organizations, professionals, and artists, Jewish American women have blended the experiences of their Jewish heritage with the fluid opportunities of the American environment.

America in the twentieth-century provided the political and economic climate for Jews to shape their own destiny. Bright and energetic Jewish women joined their brothers in applying the words of Jeremiah and Isaiah to social evils. America gave them the impression that it could be changed for the better; indeed, that it invited its citizens to work for its betterment. Emma Goldman, Rose Pastor Stokes, and Rose Schneiderman were three outstanding Jewish women who, with the zeal of the prophets and the stamina of secular reformers, assumed that charge.

This study focuses upon Jewish American women who lived public lives in both worlds. It is a selective discussion of those outstanding women and their organizations that were inspired by Judaism in their life's work. Often, they interpreted their Judaism creatively and imaginatively; at other times, they took its teachings literally and applied them to the American environment. *"Consecrate every day"* was Hannah Greenebaum Solomon's injunction to her followers in the National Council of Jewish Women. Each day should be lived with appreciation of its preciousness; each day a Jewish woman should impose her devotion to life's sacredness upon her surroundings.

The Jewish American women in this study worked out a synthesis between their Judaism and their Americanism. They comfortably retained an identity in both worlds. In the case of the radicals, their inspiration was Judaism but their identity was as citizens of the world. They are included because of their conscious ties with the Jewish community for support and sustenance. Most of the women described acted through the Jewish community; that is, they carried out their ambitions, their talents, and their hopes within the Jewish American community. In this way, they retained their clear connections with their Jewish culture while fulfilling their individual ambitions.

In the Hebrew language, there is no word for charity; the closest word is *tzdakah*, meaning "righteousness." It was not an act of good-will for a Jew to help another Jew; it was his obligation. The ancient prophets preached social responsibility: every Jew should care for every other Jew, and the pragmatic demands of poor Jews, of orphans and of widows, required the practice of *tzdakah*. It is a good deed in the Jewish religion to feed a stranger on a holiday; it is a necessity to help a fellow Jew to survive in the precarious Christian world. As the Jews adjusted to their American home, they also participated in philanthropic activities within a larger community. So while Jews continued to support Jewish social-welfare causes, they also contributed to the local art museum, symphony orchestra, and community chest.

Although the words of *tzdakah* were usually directed to the males in the congregation, Jewish women listened, heard, and heeded the moral strictures of their rabbis. Many Jewish women demonstrated their fervor and devotion to Judaism by their good works. While Jewish women might not be counted in the praying number (the *min-yan*) in the synagogue, called to the Torah to read a blessing, or receive an honor on a holiday, they practiced their Judaism through their synagogue's sisterhood, through organizations such as the National Council of Jewish Women, and through the programs provided for the Jewish elderly, the orphans, and the destitute. Similarly, the wives of Jewish Socialists, secularists, and intelligentsia listened to their husbands discuss the ills of American industrial society and then became active leaders in unions; they also led strikes and lectured to the community. Jewish American women, whether they were religiously observant or cultural Jews, created their own particular parallel structures and forms within which to express their Jewish concerns.

The Jewish American women in this study represent the broad spectrum of American Judaism. Some claimed a connection to a secular, Socialist-Yiddish heritage; others were raised in a religious environment. Still others viewed themselves as Jews though their knowledge of Jewish history or literature was minimal. All of these women established a conscious connection with Jewish people, Jewish causes, and Jewish themes. Their self-definition included their Judaism. In the case of a Jewish woman writer such as Edna Ferber, the Christian community acted as a constant reminder to a little Jewish girl in Appleton, Wisconsin that she was different from them. The intriguing factor that unifies all of the women and all of their work is their conscious effort to integrate their Judaism with their personal ambition and their commitment to secular American values. These Jewish American women created unique syntheses, original ways of blending the best of two vital traditions.

It is the public life of people to which the historian has the greatest access. The Jewish woman's domestic life, if she was a practicing Jew, was regulated by the religious calendar. In addition to the regular, repetitive chores required in running a household, she prepared for the Sabbath every Friday and baked the proper delicacies before each holiday. When working-class and middle-class Jewish women left their homes to work or to volunteer their services to the community, their lives took on another dimension, one that was recorded in public documents, and one that called them to the attention of the society at large. The story of Jewish women's public lives has yet to be told. The following pages are a modest contribution to that effort.

While the last two decades of the nineteenth century form the backdrop for *Consecrate Every Day*, the primary focus is upon the twentieth century. There are at least four generations of Jewish American women under consideration. While the complex religious culture of Judaism remains an active ingredient in their lives, these women have blended that ingredient with the more flexible educational, ideological, and economic climate of America. Jewish women have tested and reshaped the traditional sex-role divisions in this country more than any other ethnic group. In the 1970's, Jewish women attained higher levels of education as a group than American women in general. Today they play prominent roles in the professions, in reform organizations, and in the creative arts. This is so, it seems to me, because they have selected, in a healthy, eclectic fashion, the qualities in both cultures that encourage human development. They have applied the rhetoric of individual rights and equal opportunity to themselves.

The Jewish American women included in this book were selected because of their active, visible ties to the Jewish community. The volunteer activists belonged to Jewish organizations, while the writers expressed Jewish themes in their work. It is the broad, conscious connection with Jewish culture, not just the Jewish religion, that is of concern here. Writers who happened to be Jewish but did not write about the Jewish experience (or the personal experiences of being Jewish) are not included. Social reformers who were born

Jews but for whom Jewish organizations and causes were irrelevant are not included either. As will be described later, a Jewish woman rebel such as Emma Goldman never forgot nor abandoned her connection with Judaism; that is why she is included in this study. She rejected the Jewish religion but always identified as a Jew and sought out Jewish audiences for her speeches.

Women are defined in Western society, by both Jews and Christians, according to the position of their fathers or husbands, not by their own public lives. Thus, women who work professionally outside of the home act out roles other than the one determining and predictable role for all adult women. Middle- and upper-class women, of course, have found that society approves of their philanthropic, volunteer activities as they fulfill the helpmate and nurturing dimensions of the wifely role. Jewish women who helped their husbands in their retail businesses shared with their husbands and their culture the view that their "work" was not as important as their wifely and motherly work. Jewish women who formed auxiliaries to the men's benevolent societies accepted the cultural view that women were followers, not leaders; helpmates, not initiators. Indeed, it is only a few Jewish women who rebelled against the dominant value system and created new role definitions for themselves. The public life of Jewish American women has been rich and impressive but, for the most part, it has been within culturally approved boundaries. What Jewish American women have done is to test, and, sometimes, stretch the boundaries. The bold rebels, as Emma Goldman quickly discovered, lead a perilous life in a traditional culture.

But no analysis should demean or belittle the important contributions of the "volunteer activists." They, their cohorts, and their beneficiaries all profited from the interaction. Although society never criticized the good works of the volunteer activists, it rarely praised them either. These women maintained a harmonious balance between their public activities and their domestic obligations. They remained good wives and often had husbands who supported their work. Self-fulfillment, social satisfaction, and self-sacrifice intermingled in subtle and important ways in their lives.

Jewish immigrant women workers are included in this discussion because out of their experiences emerged an active labor-union effort by many women. The sweatshop was the training ground for Jewish women leaders. While American women have not yet become leaders in great numbers in labor unions, Jewish women stood out as fearless leaders in the early days of union organizing. The exploitation of the workers in the garment industry cried out for reformation and it was Jewish women workers who responded. Indeed, it was the women workers who organized and struck before the men workers gathered their courage to do likewise in the garment industry. The spunkiness and sheer daring displayed by the Jewish women workers early in the century foreshadowed their continued reaction to injustice in America. The first generation of twentieth-century Jewish American women took charge of their own lives and acted for the common good.

The ingredients of American culture meshed with the Jewish culture in the first major meeting of the two at the end of the nineteenth century (when mass Jewish migration began). A politically democratic environment, a period of expanding, individualistically oriented capitalism, and a rhetoric of individual freedom, all American values and realities, were compatible with the social philosophy of Judaism. Although America's words and actions did not always blend, the sentiments of the Declaration of Independence, protected by the Constitution, enabled white people, even Jewish immigrants, to seize economic opportunities, to feel protected by their citizenship rights, and to practice their religion freely. The American experience of tolerating differences, based upon the practical necessity of integrating a very heterogeneous population of immigrants, enabled Jews to succeed within the American culture.

Both Americans and Jews understood what it meant to be underdogs, to come from behind, and to applaud individual effort. WASP values harmonized with Jewish values. Indeed, Jewish Americans became great examples of Horatio Alger and Benjamin Franklin types. Both Jews and Christian Americans admired loyalty to family and community; both groups believed that individuals were responsible for their fate; and both believed that it was morally imperative that a group care for the welfare of others.

The marvelous accomplishment of American history has been its ability to preserve primary identities in diverse subcultures while providing an American umbrella under which all ethnic groups, all religions, and all value systems could operate. Jewishness has remained the primary identity network for most Jewish Americans, while the American environment and culture offers a variety of secondary and tertiary associations. Jewish Americans can attend the synagogue and a ballgame, a Jewish community center activity and a university-sponsored lecture on Lord Byron. Both the particular and the universal can be easily managed in diversity-rich America.

Jewish American women, at least those discussed as examples and representatives in this book, have applied the American concept of public education for both sexes to themselves. Scholarship had always been a Jewish value, but only in America could Jewish girls attend classes with Jewish boys. The rhetoric of rugged individualism, a peculiarly American idea, has had many unanticipated consequences for Jewish women—indeed, for all American women. Never before the second half of the twentieth century has the rhetoric of individualism been employed by women for themselves. The family has always been the woman's primary unit, Jewish and Christian alike. A woman's sense of self was derived from her husband's economic class and status; her adult occupation was marriage and child rearing. Only since the 1960's have large numbers of Jewish and Christian women explored the concept of individualism and declared that it also applies to them.

Jewish women, raised in a culture that encouraged learning, individual decision making, and pride in accomplishment were galvanized by the heady words of the Declaration of Independence into leadership positions in the women's liberation, mental health, and anti-war movements. Jewish American women were among the major articulators of the new definitions of womanhood. They were among the first to test the boundaries among family, self-development, and community. They were enthusiastic volunteers in social-service agencies and then leading critics of the woman-as-unpaid-labor syndrome. How did Jewish American women come to their present questioning? How did they evolve as accurate bellwethers of the dilemmas facing all American women? What have been their working, cultural, and professional roles in twentieth-century America? *Consecrate Every Day* tries to deal with these questions and offer some tentative answers.

This study is based largely on secondary sources. It is a synthesis, hopefully an unusual one, of disparate materials that have not been brought together in this way before. It offers a selective look at key Jewish women, not a comprehensive, all-inclusive view. In all cases, however, I explain why I have selected particular women and themes; I hope the reader will share my questions and concerns. One may find innumerable other examples of worthy women and organizations to include, but this book offers a part of the very fascinating story of Jewish American women.

2. Jewish Women Workers

When contemporary Americans think about Jewish women, they rarely think of them as factory workers, women who spent sixty hours a week in sweatshops where the doors were locked from the outside. Yet this was a reality for thousands of European Jewish women immigrants in the early twentieth century. Jewish women worked on rented sewing machines with thread they paid for out of their meager wages. Unskilled and poor, these young Jewish women left home to seek employment not in schools or settlement houses or hospitals, but in factories sewing shirtwaists, caps, dresses, and underwear. By 1900, over fifty-three percent of all employed Jewish women worked in the garment industry, an industry that was overwhelmingly owned by Jewish manufacturers.[1] These Jewish employers showed no particular sympathy or kindness to their coreligionists. The hours were long, the pay low, and the conditions deplorable.

The young, unmarried Jewish immigrant women who worked in the garment industry early in this century became the mothers and grandmothers of the educated, ambitious Jewish women of the 1960s and 1970s. They knew how difficult the dream of equal opportunity was to obtain. Through hard work, many of them experienced the joy of starting their own business with their husband and of giving their children an economically easier life than they had had. Individual hard work, self-discipline, self-denial, and hope for the future, all American and Jewish values, became part of their daily experience. They lived largely in their self-contained communities on the Lower East Side of New York or the near West Side of Chicago, and practiced a modified form of Judaism which they created in the new American environment.

Many young Jewish women had learned to sew in Russia and found their skill useful in America. Those without skills learned quickly, especially with the new machines that simplified the tasks. The young women, often ranging in age from sixteen to twenty, were indispensable economic aids to their families. They were earnest workers, much to the delight of their employers. Their earnings supplemented the paltry pay of their fathers and brothers. "Learners' " salaries averaged $3 to $4 a week while "regular" operators earned $7 to $12 a week. The young women's wages helped to send a younger brother to school, to supply the household with some necessities, and to relieve their mothers' constant concern for money.

Jewish women workers in the shirtwaist industry organized, led, and participated in the first mass strike of women workers in this country. Eighty percent of the workers in the trade were women and seventy percent were between the ages of 16 and 25.[2] Indeed, there were few men's strikes before it that equaled the "Uprising of the Twenty Thousand," as it came to be called. On November 22, 1909, a meeting was held in Cooper Union in New York City, a popular labor gathering place, to discuss the possibility of a general strike. Women workers had gone on strike in a number of shops and the question was whether the whole industry would also strike. After much discussion that led nowhere, a fifteen-year-old worker named Clara Lemlich, who was a board member of Local 25 of the Ladies Waistmakers Union, rose and said:

> I am a working girl, one of those who are on strike against intolerable conditions. I am tired of listening to speakers who talk in general terms. What we are here for is to decide whether we shall or shall not strike. I offer a resolution that a general strike be declared—now.

The hall resounded with shouts of approval. When the chairman of the meeting regained control of the crowd, he cried:

> Do you mean faith? Will you take the old Jewish oath? If I turn traitor to the cause I now pledge, may this hand wither from the arm I now raise.[3]

The workers raised their hands and took the pledge that all Jews knew. In its original version, Jews pledged not to forget Jerusalem, lest their right hand wither away. Adapted to workers in industrial America, the pledge took on new force in its new environment, while retaining the traditional devotion to Jewish group solidarity. The Jewish tradition of social justice and of banding together for mutual strength, support, and defense expressed itself in the Jewish workers' strong identification with unions.

The results of the Cooper Union meeting were astounding. Twenty thousand shirtwaist workers struck in an industry with some 32,000 workers and over 600 shops. The task of keeping the strikers out until the union obtained the desired settlement became a most difficult problem. As November turned into December, the women workers in their thin coats picketed, met regularly in their assigned meeting halls, withstood the indignities hurled at them by scabs and policemen, and often found themselves beaten up by these same people. Although Local 25, the leader of the strike, had an executive board of nine men and six women, the women quickly took charge of all aspects of the strike activity. Miss Reisen, a board member, had the awesome responsibility of keeping the 3,000 Italian women who struck with the Jewish workers from returning to their jobs. Although she did not understand a word of Italian, she sat in their meeting hall and jumped up every time someone spoke, suspecting that they were proposing to return to work. As Louis Levine, the historian of the International Ladies Garment Workers Union (ILGWU), noted:

> Miss Reisen . . . would guess what was proposed, jump to the platform and plead vociferously until she would get the Italian women to remain with her in the hall. She had to put up at first with a lot of abuse, but gradually she won the hearts of the Italian strikers. And towards the end of the strike she would report to the strike committee that she "could almost understand what the Italians were talking about."[4]

The women were assisted by the Women's Trade Union League (WTUL) of New York, a middle-class women's organization designed to aid working women, and by rich New York City women sympathetic to the working women's plight. Feminists and Socialists also supported the strikers by picketing with them and donating funds to them. Rose Schneiderman, a Jewish woman worker and organizer for the WTUL, spoke at fund rallies for the strikers; Mrs. O.H.P. Belmont donated money; Mary Dreier of the WTUL picketed; Jewish Socialist Rose Pastor Stokes spoke for the women as did feminist Ida Rauh. Often the leaders among the women workers were the best-paid women in the shop. It was their sympathy and sense of unity with their exploited sisters that made them take charge and inspire their coworkers to continue striking until every demand was won.

The strike wore on and on. It was not until February 15, 1910, that it officially ended. By that time, a number of small shops had settled separately with the union. At the strike's conclusion, the union had won a number of their demands, although not the primary one—the manufacturers refused to recognize the union and their right to bargain collectively. The manufacturers shortened the working hours and eliminated all of the hated charges on equipment, but they refused to recognize an exclusive union shop. To many labor historians, this "uprising" was a spontaneous beginning, a prelude to the more organized men's cloak makers strike of five months later. The subsequent strike, supported by 60,000 men, resulted in a permanent board of arbitration and a preferential union shop. The same features were not adopted in the women's clothing industry until 1913.

Although the women's strike did not achieve all of its aims, neither did the men's. Further, the effective organization of the women workers and their brave commitment to unionism was unprecedented. "One has to associate with these fine, high strung, intelligent and courageous girls to appreciate their moral caliber and their capacity for self-sacrifice and devotion," commented William Mailly about the women strike leaders.[5] Women workers had been ignored by male unionists. After 1910 their presence was at least known. The strikers considered their efforts successful. The employers reduced their working hours, gave them four legal holidays, agreed to talk to them regularly, and to divide work evenly during slack periods. The women had made their grievances a public issue and had won concessions from the manufacturers for the first time. The women workers congratulated themselves on the outcome of their three-month ordeal. Local 25 became the largest single garment-union local, boasting 10,000 members as a result of the strike. Although those numbers diminished in the following years, the immediate effect was one of complete loyalty to the union. Jewish labor historian Melech Epstein concluded that the women's strike "inspired the men at the head of the ILGWU, made overcautious by past experience, to choose a daring, new course."[6] Unfortunately, neither the women nor the men workers could sustain that solid unity, and unionism still had a long way to go before obtaining recognition in this country.

Working conditions in the shirtwaist and dressmaking industry remained precarious. Even in the large companies with newer facilities, catastrophes occurred. The following year, on March 25,

1911, a fire broke out at the Triangle Shirtwaist Company, one of the largest factories on the Lower East Side and one of the companies most resistant to unionism. One hundred-forty-six young women lost their lives in that fire, mainly because the doors of the factory had been locked from the outside and the women jumped out of the windows in a desperate attempt to save themselves. There was a single ladder leading to a narrow rear court that served as a fire escape. The *New York World* described the scene in this way:

> The first signs that persons in the street knew that these three top stories had turned into red furnaces in which human creatures were being caught and incinerated was when screaming men and women and boys and girls threw themselves into the streets far below. They jumped with their clothing ablaze. The hair of some of the girls streamed up aflame as they leaped. Thud after thud sounded on the pavements.[7]

Public cries led to more vigorous factory-inspection laws; Triangle executives claimed that their building was fireproof and they could not understand how the fire occurred. The industry did little thereafter to improve working conditions. Wages remained low, fifty-two-hour weeks continued to prevail, and workers earning $12 a week had to figure out how they were to live in a city where experts claimed that a minimum income of $18 a week was essential for survival. Neither the Ladies Shirtwaist Union nor the men's Cloakmakers Union succeeded in changing their industry's miserable conditions.

Contemporary Yiddish writers often captured the hardships and the struggles of the Jewish women workers. Abraham Reisin's story "Save Your Dimes" described how two young working women named Rose and Bertha each bought savings boxes. They resolved to save a dime rather than go to the moving-picture show or eat a special treat. After two weeks, Rose had put aside sixty cents while Bertha had saved forty cents. Before they could take pride in their thrift, they lost their jobs and Rose's savings became their food money. The story concluded:

> The broken savings-bank lay helpless on the floor like a vandalized grave. And the second bank stood on a bureau with the number 40 staring fearfully out at the world, knowing full well it was destined for the same fate as its brother on the floor. . . .[8]

Unemployment, the constant fear of unemployment, and seasonal, undependable work in the garment industry acted as a permanent cloud over the heads of all garment workers. The specter of hunger, eviction, and uncertainty never left them.

While thousands of young women bent over sewing machines in factories, thousands more worked at home sewing piecework for subcontractors who paid them for each completed piece of clothing. Reporter Jacob Riis visited one household in the early 1900s where a suspender maker and his wife and eighteen-year-old daughter worked at home, "but the girl's eyes [were] giving out from the strain."[9] Poet Edwin Markham observed that thousands of little girls remained home in what he called "home sweatshops."

> A little daughter, therefore, must assume the work and care of the family. She becomes the "little mother," washing, scrubbing, cooking. . . . Is it not a cruel civilization that allows little hearts and little shoulders to strain under these grown-up responsibilities, while in the same city a pet cur is jeweled and pampered and aired on a fine lady's velvet lap on the beautiful boulevards?[10]

It is no wonder that marriage appeared to be a salvation, an escape from the dull, hard work of the sweatshop and the home, to many young women. As Viola Paradise, a worker for Chicago's Immigrant Protective League who visited nearly 2,000 immigrant girls in the early 1910s observed:

> The chief ambition of the Jewish immigrant girl is to marry—perhaps we should not call it ambition, rather it is her hope, her expectation. It is one of her chief reasons for coming to America. She is quite frank and dignified about it, and not very sentimental.[11]

The overwhelming majority of young women workers left the factories upon marriage in their early twenties and were replaced by other young women. This may partly explain why women rarely maintained leadership positions in the unions. They remained temporary workers: in 1924, 63.8 percent of the membership of the ILGWU was made up of foreign-born Jews, while the union's women workers had decreased to 38.7 percent.[12] Further, while the fifteen-member Executive Board of Local 25 had had six women members in 1909, the ILGWU's seventeen-person board had only one woman member in 1924, Fannia M. Cohn.

Marriage, of course, did not free the Jewish woman from work. If she did not remain in the sweatshop, she sewed at home, took in boarders, or helped her husband in his small business if he was fortunate enough to have one. "In the four-room apartments," observed one commentator on the tenements of the Jewish ghetto on the Lower East Side, "one bed-room is usually sublet to one or more, frequently to two men or women, and in many houses the front room is also sublet to two or more lodgers for sleeping purposes."[13] In Chicago, observers estimated that at least twenty-five percent of all Jewish ghetto families had boarders.[14] The life of the Jewish immigrant working-class family did not miraculously become perfect and free of worries in America. As Elias Tcherikower said: "The sweatshop and the tenement were the cemeteries in which the dreams about the "goldene medine" ["golden land"] were laid to rest."[15]

Although the sweatshop and the tenement remained the bleak reality for large numbers of Jewish women, many harbored the secret hope that their children's lives would be better, less harsh, and more rewarding than their own. Some comforted themselves with their devotion to an omnipotent God who would right all wrongs someday; others took pride in their modest synagogal efforts to ease the burden of the sick and the poor. *Landsmanshaften*, family circles made up of people who came from the same European community, raised money for the burial of the poor, for hospital care, and for orphanages. No matter how poor a Jew was, he or she was expected to give *Tzdakah* for those even less fortunate.

Jewish women garment makers usually encouraged their daughters to learn secretarial skills so that they would not have to follow them into the garment factories. Indeed, the statistics suggest that within one generation, Jewish women's membership in the garment industry decreased significantly. The daughters of the immigrant women became salesclerks and secretaries. As one writer noted: "American-born girls did not take their mothers' places in the shop."[16]

It was precisely the American environment of expanding industrialization, urban growth, and political freedom that encouraged Jewish women to believe that at last, in America, they had found a home where they could be Jewish, economically prosperous, and free of overt persecution. Surely anti-Semitism or the fear of anti-

Semitism always remained a concern, but they witnessed in their own lives and in the lives of family members upward mobility as well as the hope for a better future. So the daughters of sweatshop workers rejected the working-class occupation of their mothers and chose American occupations as testimony to their conviction that their lives *would* be better.

A small, exceptional group of Jewish women made their work their life's profession: they became union leaders, an occupation that separated them from both traditional Jewish and Gentile expectations for women. Jewish and Christian employers were outraged by unions, union organizers, and especially women organizers. Women were expected by the whole business community to be docile workers, obedient to the will of the male bosses. Women workers received less pay than men for the same work and were expected to continue to do so. Considering the unpopularity of unions, it was especially bold for a Jewish woman to make a career in union activities.

Union leaders Rose Schneiderman, Pauline Newman, Fannia Cohn, and Bessie Abramowitz stood out as courageous women willing to incur the wrath of company bullies, Pinkerton police, and local police in their determined efforts to organize laboring women and men. They accepted the rhetoric of America, the faith in freedom and liberty, and the right to express their unpopular points of view. They used the strike as a weapon while also engaging in speech making, pamphleteering, and fund raising, all tried and true tools of American reformists. Often they spoke in Yiddish to their largely Jewish constituents and appealed to them with examples from the Bible and Talmud. They reminded the workers that as Jews and as Americans they were entitled to justice and a fair deal. Perhaps the most spectacular piece of evidence of the Jewish women's faith in America was their willingness to *demand* justice without fear of being personally harmed because they were Jews. Jewish assertiveness in America is the most dramatic confirmation of Jews' belief in the democratic practices of their new country, a belief so different from the attitudes created by their Old World experience.

New York City Jews knew Pauline Newman's work for the ILGWU. As the first woman organizer following the 1909 women's strike, Newman visited garment factories and recruited women for membership in the union. In 1913, she became the executive secretary of the Joint Board of Sanitary Control, the structure created to negotiate all labor disputes between the garment manufacturers and the workers. In 1919, when the Board was abandoned, the ILGWU formed the Unity Health Center to provide medical services for its members. Pauline Newman became the educational director and remained at the Center for many years. Indeed, she was recently honored by the union for her long years of devotion. The Unity Health Center, the first institution of its kind, provided social services to its union members and later an extensive program in preventive medicine administered by Pauline Newman.

In contrast, Rose Schneiderman's first organizing work came under the auspices of the Women's Trade Union League (WTUL), a largely Protestant, middle-class women's organization designed to recruit women for the existing unions. Led by Mrs. Raymond Robbins and supported by many wealthy New York women, the WTUL tried to educate women to the need for union membership. Schneiderman recruited Barnard College students to help women strikers during the 1909 strike.[17] She became the president of the New York branch of the WTUL, a job she retained for many years. Schneiderman's connections with working women extended to the ILGWU as well as the WTUL. She consulted with Pauline Newman and understood the problems of immigrant working women from firsthand experience. Before becoming a union organizer, Schneiderman, herself an immigrant from Russian Poland, worked in a cap-making factory and a department store.

The problems of being a Jewish woman organizer working in the WTUL, a Christian organization, concerned Rose Schneiderman. In correspondence and discussions with Pauline Newman, Schneiderman deliberated over whether the Protestant women of the WTUL understood the particular needs and problems of Jewish working women. Newman cautioned Schneiderman in one letter: "Remember Rose, that no matter how much you are with the Jewish people, you are still more with the people of the League." And in another letter in 1912, she stated: "They don't understand the difference between the Jewish girl and the gentile girl."[18]

Newman's concerns appeared to be stronger than Schneiderman's who continued to work with the WTUL while organizing Jewish garment workers. The union became the vital institution, the organization which would improve the standard of living for all workers, and Schneiderman remained committed to it all her life. Although she was Jewish and her cultural connections remained with Jews, she maintained a cooperative relationship with the WASP WTUL. In the 1930s, Rose Schneiderman became the only female member of

Franklin Roosevelt's National Labor Relations Board; from 1937 to 1944, she was secretary of the New York Department of Labor. Schneiderman always believed in the need for educating women so that they would use their political and economic power intelligently. "Women shirk the responsibility for decisive action on public questions," she once said. "And it is not surprising. For so many hundreds of years they haven't been held responsible for anything outside their own households."[19]

The only other first-generation union woman who achieved a leadership position in the ILGWU and devoted her life to it was Fannia Cohn, the ILGWU's only woman vice-president in 1916. Two years later, she became secretary of the ILGWU's Educational Committee. In this capacity, she organized Unity House, a retreat for workers, and numerous Unity Centers where classes for workers were held. A Workers University was also part of the educational program. One contemporary commentator noted that Cohn "bridged the gulf that generally exists between the college professor and the trade unionist and enabled them to understand one another."[20]

Fannia Cohn also worked closely with the writers and editors of *Justice*, the union's magazine. Although working women were very grateful for the humanizing and intellectually exciting dimensions introduced into the union by Cohn, many male unionists considered Unity House and its classes frivolities. But the union kept these activities and eventually became proud to point to them as signs of their progressive nature.[21] Fannia Cohn felt that "the union's activities should influence every possible phase of the worker's life."[22]

Cohn's commitment to the ILGWU and to education topped her list of priorities. Jewish workers made up her original constituency, but they were replaced over the years with other ethnic groups. Cohn's devotion to the union superseded all others. This organization, which provided her with a career, an identity, and a world view, occupied the place of family and community. As a woman, she sacrificed the traditional Jewish woman's roles to become a full-time unionist. Whether this was a conscious decision or not is not revealed in the written records.

Although most accounts of early unionizing efforts focus upon New York City's garment industry, the very same scenario was taking place in other cities such as Chicago, Philadelphia, and Cleveland. Because striking and unionizing were becoming more frequent activities as working conditions deteriorated and because women workers dominated the garment industry, women were important leaders and foot soldiers in the fights for unionization. In

Chicago in 1910 a very spunky Jewish woman led a strike against the garment manufacturers Hart, Schaffner and Marx. Her name was Bessie Abramowitz and she led her coworkers out of the factory when the piece rate for seaming pants was lowered from four cents to three-and-three-fourths cents per piece. Within a short period of time, she and her cohorts were joined by most of the 8,000 workers at the company.

Before long, 40,000 other workers in the men's garment industry had also struck. Only twenty years old, Bessie Abramowitz was already an experienced worker and labor leader. A few years earlier, she had been fired from another Chicago sweatshop for protesting when a foreman scratched out her work rate on her work sheet and lowered the piece rate. The Chicago clothing manufacturers blacklisted her as a troublemaker and she had to leave the city in order to find work. She returned a year later and, under an assumed name, got a job at Hart, Schaffner and Marx.[23]

Bessie Abramowitz displayed great energy and skill in organizing. She worked for the Women's Trade Union League in Chicago to organize the women at Hart, Schaffner and Marx for the United Garment Workers Union. She soon became the head of the vest makers' local at the company. She worked effectively with another young labor leader, Sidney Hillman, and eventually played a major role in helping him become the president of the Amalgamated Clothing Workers of America. In fact, their admiration for each other's abilities blossomed into romance; after a long courtship, they married in 1916. By this time, Hillman's Amalgamated had become a fast-growing union and the couple settled in New York.

Bessie Abramowitz, although continuing to take an interest in union activities, devoted herself to raising a family. Her behavior effectively summarized what became the pattern of most women union activists. Marriage and children removed them from continued involvement. Newman, Cohn, and Schneiderman remained single while Abramowitz, an equally impressive union leader, chose to give up her career for home and family. The evidence suggests that this decision was a happy and satisfying one; but it aptly displayed the dominant Jewish and American values toward women: single women might be tolerated in the work force, even in leadership positions, but married women should be home with their children. Male union leaders, by all accounts, shared this value system.

In discussions about their work and experiences, all of these union leaders acknowledged that doing battle with employers, facing hostile crowds, and trying to convince reluctant women workers of the virtues of the union made them self-confident, independent, and self-determining women. Their Jewish heritage inspired them to fight against social injustice and to work for economic righteousness. They drew inspiration from Jewish writings that emphasized human dignity and the obligation to speak out against evil. Their audience, their constituency, for most of their activities was made up of Jews who shared their general perspective.

While few Jewish women workers made the union their profession, many working-class Jewish women devoted time and energy to benevolent and philanthropic work within their community. Families brought relatives over from Europe, organized cousins clubs, and participated in a variety of social, cultural, and educational activities. The *vereins* or *chevras*, as they were called in Yiddish, paralleled other communal efforts of social service. These groups often met in the home of the *Landsfroy* [the woman from the Russian village].[24] Some groups were named after women; some examples were the Golde Goldman Cousin and Family Circle, the Debora Halberstam, Lewi Cousin and Family Circle, and the Betty Weiss Cousin and Family Circle.[25] These groups of like-minded people socialized and paid dues for future uses such as burial costs, insurance, and charity.

In addition to these clubs there were *landsmanshaften*, run by the men. As these grew in size and number, the women formed Ladies Auxiliary Societies, ancillary organizations to their husbands' *landsmanshaften*. In 1938 there were over 200 Ladies Auxiliaries, and one study claims that almost a half a million people belonged to *landsmanshaften* in New York City. This number represented one out of every four Jews in the city.[26] The Auxilaries also contributed to national organizations such as the Hebrew Immigrant Aid Society and the American Jewish Joint Distribution Committee.[27] Their efforts were appreciated by the men's societies. Male secretaries sometimes aided the ladies, and one such person noted in the introduction to the constitution of the Mezrichter Ladies' Aid Society:

We may now consider our Farain a large growing family. We are confident that our *Mezrichter Ladies Aid Society* will continue its existence for ever and always. Our experience has taught us to value and respect the many good deeds and work of our farain. We must therefore maintain our sacred duty to support our rules, so that our "sister-love" may under no circumstance be disrupted.[28]

From the close allegiance between the Ladies Auxiliaries and the men's organizations, one can gather that these women's groups did not establish independent identities or carve out new purposes. They accepted male leadership and performed the social and charitable duties required of them.

Like their middle- and upper-class sisters, working-class Jewish women held teas to raise money for a local orphan, dances to provide funds for insurance benefits, and lectures to enlighten everyone. On these occasions they dressed in their best clothes and socialized with their fellow countrymen. Working-class Jewish women, therefore, participated and often led in the social structures created by their community. This first generation's actions provided the foundation for all future generations of Jewish American women's social-service work in the Jewish community.

Another response to the hard life of the garment workers was to cultivate all of the American and Jewish communal resources that would enable them, and their children, to surmount the factory. A noted characteristic among Jewish working girls was their tremendous devotion to American and Jewish culture in all of its forms. Social worker Viola Paradise observed that the young Jewish woman was the most eager immigrant to Americanize: "with no other nationality does the Americanizing process begin so soon, and continue so consciously."[29] The desire to become an American, to participate in the material abundance, the social advancement, and the cultural opportunities of America excited and intrigued the young Jewish woman. She also wanted to be like the native American women she saw around her. "She is quick," Paradise continued, "to accept the conventional; she is willing to be better than her neighbor but she dreads being different."[30] Although some Jewish critics viewed the rapid assimilation of young Jewish women as detrimental to Jewish survival, this behavior can also be interpreted as a healthy effort to enjoy the new freedoms of American life.

One display of the women's desire for self-betterment was their large attendance at numerous Americanization classes, English classes, cultural lectures, and vocational-training classes. If the women lived on New York City's Lower East Side, the home of hundreds of thousands of immigrant Jews, they attended classes at the Henry Street Settlement House, the Educational Alliance, and numerous other facilities. They learned millinery work, nursing, and business skills. The Women's Auxiliary of the Educational Alliance and the National Council of Jewish Women in New York, Chicago, Philadelphia and elsewhere conducted educational classes for immigrant women. In Chicago, the Maxwell Street Settlement House and Hull House were also popular. Each city with a substantial Jewish immigrant population had similar institutions.

Autobiographical memoirs often provide us with the clues we need to understand human values and motivations. Young Jewish women, raised in a culture that respected male learning, discovered that, in America, Jewish girls could share in the joys of intellectual activity. One daughter of immigrants, Elizabeth Stern, described her parents: "To my father and mother all the universe was bound by their religious affiliations and by memories of the old land left behind."[31] Stern's father resisted her pleadings to go to high school because he feared that increased education would take the young woman out of the Jewish community, raise her expectations, and separate her from her traditional family ties. Stern's mother supported her daughter's eagerness to attend high school, and so she went. The father's fears, in fact, were realized: Stern married a Christian and disassociated herself from her family. But to Elizabeth Stern, the promise of America was a promise for individual development for advancing beyond traditional barriers, and for becoming an American citizen, not just a Jew. Her mother identified with her yearnings and encouraged her; in America, girls as well as boys could receive an education, although the costs and risks were different.

Immigrant Mary Antin wrote in her memoir:

When the rebbe (teacher) came on Sabbath afternoon, to examine the boy in the hearing of the family, everybody sat around the table and nodded with satisfaction, if he read his portion well; and he was given a great saucerful of preserves, and was praised, and blessed, and made much of. No wonder he said in his morning prayer, "I thank Thee, Lord, for not having created me a female." It was not much fun to be a girl . . . . Girls could not be scholars. . . .[32]

It is no wonder, then, that young working women satisfied their intellectual yearnings in the settlement-house classes and in secular cultural activities. Traditional Judaism did not provide for their intellectual growth, so they sought elsewhere in the first country that gave them the opportunity to study.

Jewish boys had to learn Torah, attend Hebrew school, study for the Bar Mitzvah ceremony, and become active participants in synagogue activities. Women were not accepted in the praying number needed to conduct a prayer service. It was assumed that Jewish girls learned all they had to know to run a proper Jewish home from their mothers. Formal education was unnecessary. Thus, immigrant Jews in America provided little religious education for their daughters. Rabbi Isaac Mayer Wise, a leader of American Reform Judaism, wrote:

> The Jewish woman had been treated almost as a stranger in the synagogue; she had been kept at a distance, and had been excluded from any participation in the life of the congregation . . .[33]

In the early part of the century one reporter summed up the situation in Chicago as follows: "What is being done for the religious needs of the children of the district? For the boys much, for the girls comparatively little."[34]

Jewish women, in their quest for intellectual stimulation, devoured the Yiddish newspapers. They read the *Jewish Daily Forwards*, the largest Yiddish newspaper, and wrote letters to its popular advice column, the "Bintele Brief" [Bundles of letters]. Young Jewish women asked about American dating practices, intermarriage, and the problems of married people. According to one source, the overwhelming majority of readers were under twenty-five years old.[35] Women asked how they could motivate a lazy husband and how to deal with rebellious children. Immigrant women attended the Yiddish theater with their husbands and children and thrilled to the performances of Boris Thomaschevsky, Maurice Schwartz, Bertha Kalish, and others. They loved watching a performance of *Mirele Efros*, the story of a female King Lear, and they cried over the tribulations of a Jewish mother with ungrateful children. They rioted after seeing a Yiddish performance of Ibsen's *Doll House*.[36] When Nora walked out in the fourth act, the Jewish women cheered.

Socialist women also spent time at the innumerable coffee shops in their neighborhoods debating the evils of capitalism with their male cohorts. For those who remained observant Jews, the ritual demands of the synagogue and the home occupied them as well. During the summers, working-class Jewish families went to the Catskill Mountains for their vacations. Wives and children would leave the city for a few weeks, and be joined by their husbands on the weekends. One contemporary observer noted:

. . . The vacation habit is unquestionably stronger among the Jewish poor than among any other class. One would never think of an Italian laborer or an Irishman working on a street railroad, sending his wife and children away for the summer. Yet, the Jewish sweatshop worker does this, year after year, for he has learned that it saves much illness in the fall and winter. Besides, it gives him a well earned rest. . .[37]

Another good example of the Americanization of the immigrant Jewish women was the interest in discovering effective methods of birth control. The Comstock law prevented the distribution of information or devices, but desperate immigrant women with large families defied both the Comstock law and traditional Jewish law, which commanded them to "be fruitful and multiply." Jewish working-class women read Margaret Sanger's *What Every Woman Should Know* in Yiddish. As late as 1930, discussions of women's sex lives were written in Yiddish.[38] Immigrant Jewish families were large, though the infant-mortality rate was also high. As one writer said: "Mother became a mother eleven times. Only the four children lived."[39] Abortion also was practiced by women with already large families. Both Emma Goldman and Margaret Sanger acted as nurses on the Lower East Side; they visited crowded tenement homes of immigrants, helped the women give birth, and also helped to save their lives after unsuccessful abortions.

The matchmaker, or *schadchen* as he was called in Yiddish, complained that his business was declining in America. The daughters of immigrants insisted upon choosing their own husbands. They dressed like American girls, went to vaudeville houses rather than the Yiddish theater, and aspired to a middle-class American life. Indeed, as early as 1921, one commentator in the *Jewish Forum* complained that Jewish women were drifting away from the synagogue and home observance.

There is no time for the Sabbath reception, as her boys "must" attend the boy scout meeting while the girls must attend one or the other of the mediocre social "events," a musicale or a dance which, counting on the lack of backbone of the modern Jewish mother, her Gentile friends invariably arrange for Friday evenings.[40]

In their pursuit of middle-class American respectability, many

Jewish women discarded not only their memories of sweatshop life but of religious observance as well, a phenomenon often noted by traditionalist critics.

By the early 1920s, between 20,000 and 30,000 young women worked in the dry-goods and department stores of New York City, with fully one-third of them being Jewish.[41] The wages were low but this work was viewed as a cut higher than the factory. The women dressed better, met the public, and hoped for advancement into more dignified jobs and lives. Viola Paradise astutely noted that the working girl's "desires increased far more rapidly than her income."[42] Making a desirable marriage, one that guaranteed financial security, became the understandable dream. These young women had known the miserable life of the garment factory and the humdrum existence of the retail store. Being women, they knew that few lucrative job oportunities existed for them. American women, Jewish and Christian, were raised to believe that their adult lives were to be lived as wives and mothers. Jewish women could work in their husbands' business, as all women should be dutiful helpmates. But otherwise, working outside of the home was to be a temporary activity, unless misfortune struck and doomed them to spinsterhood or widowhood.

Jewish women workers in the early twentieth century led their public lives in America. They were the first generation to experience in large numbers the evils of sweatshop capitalism as well as the joy of leaving the factory. Most young women left upon marriage and worked either at home or in their husbands' business. They exulted in the materialistic opportunities of expanding America. They gained self-confidence as a result of their working, their union activities, and their cultural experiences. In these ways, they absorbed the values of entrepreneurial America, of the virtues and rewards of hard work, and the benefits of a tolerant political environment. Freed from the constant worry of survival in Eastern Europe, the Jewish American immigrant woman could plan better futures for her children because she saw measurable improvement in her own life.

Except for the few Jewish women who became union leaders, most remained traditional Jewish women in that they defined themselves as women in the same way that Jewish culture did. They favored their sons' education over their daughters; they expected all of their children to marry and have children; and they utilized their considerable energy and organizational skill by volunteering their services to their synagogue's sisterhood, the newly formed Hadassah, the local Jewish hospital, and the family circle. They channeled their personal ambition into helping their families achieve success. They stood behind their husbands, sometimes exhibiting false modesty when others praised them for their husbands' accomplishments. Their public lives as workers and as community builders established the foundation for all future generations.

3. Inspired by Judaism: Radical Jewish Women Activists

People raised within the Jewish fold, like people raised within any religious culture, have a number of choices regarding their relationship to that religion: they may actively follow its tenets, actively reject them, passively step away from them, or selectively practice them. Most people, I think, fall into the last category. The zealous carry out all of the religious principles with enthusiasm and precision; the rebellious few defy religion with equal zeal. The conscious rejectors of Judaism eat pork boldly and rebuke the rituals that they had once practiced. In so doing, they still remain captive to the tradition they reject.

The nature of their rebellion is dictated by their Jewishness. For some rebels who stepped away from Judaism, secular concerns took on the proportions of a religion. Many Jewish Socialists, for example, embraced Marxism with religious fervor. Often, they borrowed ideas, vocabulary, and values from their old religion and adapted them to their new one. The passive nonpractitioners adopted other creeds, dogmas, or codes, or they lived according to secular American values that preached fair play, rugged individualism, and rooting for the underdog.

Even Jewish rebels whose overt actions seemed totally unrelated to Judaism were, I submit, connected with the Jewish, particularly the prophetic, tradition. As products of a religious culture that saw all human fates as intertwined, they inevitably looked at the world from that perspective. The Jewish environment might be repressed or ignored in the pursuit of other gods, but its existence, as the starting point of the Jew, could never be totally erased. This assumption, of course, is difficult to document. Thus, the following discussion will concentrate on Jewish women rebels whose words and actions demonstrated their Jewish background and their ties to the Judaic tradition. Their public lives became bold expressions of discontent with the status quo. These women rebels departed from Judaism in the sense that they no longer observed Jewish rituals or holiday ceremonies. Further, their self-identities, though not excluding their Jewish origins, did not rest upon Judaism either. Jewish women rebels were often workers, like the women described in the previous chapter, but their philosophical commitment to socialism, anarchism, or Communism set them apart from the religious Jewish community and strained relations with the traditionalists. These women displayed a wholeness, a sense of self-confidence and esteem, that is truly rare to behold in women of any period. They were sure of themselves and of their convictions.

Allen Guttmann, in his book *The Jewish Writer in America*, discussed the Jewish radical male as a marginal man; he was outside the Christian, host culture by virtue of his Jewishness. In fact, Guttmann saw the Jewish radical as doubly alienated: from Judaism as well as from the Christian bourgeois society. Within this framework, the Jewish woman rebel is triply alienated: from her religion, from the Christian culture, and from both cultures' views of women. A male radical, by criticizing the social world he lives in, is still operating within sex-role expectations—as a thinker, analyst, and activist. None of these qualities is assigned to, or expected of, females in either the Jewish or Christian tradition. Thus, a Jewish woman radical stands outside both cultures simultaneously by her rebellion.

Paradoxically, the social rebels of the early part of the century operated within the organic Jewish community. They spoke Yiddish, attended the Yiddish theater, read Yiddish literature, and generally participated in the rich Jewish cultural life of the Lower East Side of New York. The coffee shop became a familiar social gathering place for radical Socialists. Jews associated with other Jews, spoke in Yiddish, and shared a point of view. Thus, Jewish women rebels did not leave their cultural community when they departed from religious Judaism. They stopped practicing Jewish rituals and rarely, if ever, attended synagogue, but they saw their fellow Jews as their natural constituents and allies and never believed that cultural Jews could not also be social rebels. A Jewish Socialist, after all, became a significant social type among the rebels.

The immigrant Jewish working woman has been credited and blamed for instigating the uprising of the 20,000 workers in 1909 and for spreading Socialist ideas among factory workers. Indeed, it was often concrete working conditions that turned Jewish women workers to Socialism. This philosophy became a pragmatic response to deplorable factory conditions. In an analysis of letters to the "*Bintele* Brief" column of the *Jewish Daily Forward*, one writer noted:

> The socialism to which *Bintl* correspondents gave their allegiance was not exclusively, nor even primarily, an economic theory. There is little or no evidence of any sophisticated awareness of the intricacies of Marxist doctrines. Many writers protest against poverty and list detailed grievances against the capitalist class, but for the most part their socialism seems to be an ethical system rather than an economic or sociological doctrine.[1]

Most of the writers to the "Bintele Brief" column were women. As a recent study suggested, "the girls, searching and idealistic, even gave a religious cast to [radical ideas], necessary for so many in those times."[2] One observer reported on a labor meeting on the East Side and noted: "These men and women did not laugh when told of the slave girls of Egypt: they understood far too well."[3] Jewish working women were conscious of their Jewish history, conscious of the fact that Jews had been slaves in Egypt and oppressed in Russia, and singled out everywhere as Jews; thus, they mixed their Socialism with a religious fervor, a Jewish historical sense, and a moral energy unknown to most Christian working women in America.

Emma Goldman, the great anarchist lecturer and writer, spoke like a latter-day prophet and her audiences, often largely Jewish, responded with enthusiasm. Her style, her fervor, and her themes were familiar ones. The prophet Isaiah said:

> Learn to do well;
> Seek justice, relieve the oppressed,
> Judge the fatherless, plead for the widow[4]

Emma Goldman acted out this command in her long struggle for social justice in America. Charismatic rabbis were proper analogues to Goldman rather than middle-class social reformers. In her discussions of the virtues of anarchism, delivered in Yiddish, she argued that the proper religion for twentieth-century people was anarchism. Her phraseology, her moral energy, and her ethical stance were well-grounded in Judaism, a formal religion which she rejected but a spirit which she acknowledged. In principle, Emma Goldman denounced all formal religions, all formal structures that inhibited individual growth and development, but her mode of expression was distinctly Jewish.

Becoming rebels, however, was a most difficult task for Jewish women. The woman, after all, is the giver of life, the teacher of ritual to her daughters, and the moral example to the community. Obedience is a strongly emphasized virtue for women in both the Jewish and Christian traditions. For Jewish women, then, to reject their heritage by behaving in a completely unacceptable manner required enormous courage, energy, and conviction. Henrietta Szold summarized the situation well:

> Girls once brought to the point of rebellion are more radical than boys, or they appear to be. A woman's revolt affects the home, a man's the synagogue. There can be no doubt which is the more alarming and offensive. To the Jew, accustomed from time immemorial to regard Jewish women as symbols of loyalty, a daughter's insubordination is nothing short of a catastrophe.[5]

Szold, of course, was not speaking of political rebels but rather of Jewish women who rejected Jewish tradition and thus endangered the survival of the Jewish religion. This discussion centers around the minority of ideological rebels, as it would be impossible to document the larger number of Jewish women who simply did not continue to practice Jewish tradition.

Most accounts of American Jewish life ignore the ideologically rebellious Jewish woman. In discussing the trade-union movement among Jews in New York City in the early part of the century, for example, most accounts minimize the role of Jewish women. When the predominance of Socialism among immigrant Jews on the Lower East Side is described, the Jewish women Socialists are blithely overlooked. The invisibility of women is especially evident in discussions of rebels.

And yet the amazing fact is that an articulate minority of Jewish women, raised in a traditional culture questioned that tradition along with some of the men. For many radical Jewish women, Judaism required serious alterations in order to become appropriate for living in America in the twentieth century. For others, Socialism, anarchism, and feminism became the new religions, religions that spoke to their needs, their dreams, and their hopes for themselves and for all others. Some radical Jewish women rejected Judaism totally while others combined their commitment to new ideologies with their adherence to traditional Judaism. Emma Goldman best typifies the former position while Henrietta Szold, an ardent Zionist, represented the latter view.

Jewish Socialists often called attention to the fact that both Jesus and Marx were Jews, and, as noted in one fictional conversation between two Socialist women, "they were both labor leaders—both labor agitators."[6] Hutchins Hapgood, in his perceptive study of the immigrant Jews in New York early in the century, observed that many uneducated Jewish women received their education from reading and hearing Socialist propaganda on the Lower East Side.

> Many of these women, so long as they are unmarried, lead lives thoroughly devoted to "the cause," and afterwards become good wives and fruitful mothers, and urge on their husbands and sons active work in the "movement."[7]

Married Jewish women, according to Hapgood, gave up their active participation in Socialist causes, and played the traditional role of helpmate. With the few spectacular exceptions of Jewish women who remained in leadership positions, his assessment appears to be accurate. Just as the Jewish women left the leadership of the International Ladies Garment Workers Union to the men, so Socialist women gave up vigorous participation after marriage.

Another contemporary account of the Socialist coffee shops dramatically described the women present:

> And where the cigarette smoke is thickest and denunciation of the present forms of government loudest there you find women! One wishes he could write these women down gently. But to none would gentle words sound more strange than to the women of the radical coffee "parlor," who listen to strongest language, and loudest voices, nor fail to make themselves heard in the heat of the discussion.[8]

The reporter went on to describe these women as "unwomanly" in appearance: "pallid, tired, thin-lipped, flat-chested and angular, wearing men's hats and shoes, without a hint of color or finery."[9] Some of these women had heard about Socialism and trade unionism in Russia while others had their first exposure to these radical political philosophies in New York City. In both cases, the women substituted political zeal for religious zeal and brought intense commitment to the new Socialist order derived from their ancestral view of utopia.

To many Socialist Jewish women, the worker became the agent of the Messiah and the Socialist Revolution became the tool to achieve the Promised Land. Walter Rideout has commented on the connections between Judaism and Marxism:

> Both Judaism and Marxism, at least as Karl Marx conceived it, insisted on a morality of individuals free from any form of tyranny; and the social idealism and hatred of injustices found in the utterances of the best Socialist leaders resembled those of the great prophets of ancient Israel, even to some extent in phraseology.[10]

And Rose Pastor Stokes, a leading Socialist spokeswoman of the period, said:

> I believe . . . that the Jewish people, because of the ancient and historic struggle for social and economic justice, should be peculiarly fitted to recognize a special mission in the cause of the modern socialist movement . . . [11]

Stokes was a good example of a Russian Jewish immigrant raised in poverty and converted to Socialism. The daughter of a boot maker and niece to three cantors, she was raised, as one writer noted, "learning about the Torah, poverty, and emigration."[12] She recalled in her unpublished autobiography that her mother, divorced from her father when Rose was three, refused to marry her Polish lover because he was not Jewish and that was "against her father's will."[13]

Rose Pastor was a Jew aware of her religious and cultural difference from the Christian majority; in Europe and then in the United States, she experienced the discrimination reserved for Jews, especially poor Jews. At twelve years old, a new arrival in America, she went to work as a cigar maker in Cleveland and earned one dollar a week; her nimble fingers aided her and within months, she earned four dollars a week. Although she tried other jobs, she usually returned to the cigar factory, and she remained in that grueling occupation for twelve years. But Rose Pastor had literary ambitions; she wrote poetry in her native Yiddish. In 1903, the *Tageblatt*, (*The New York Jewish Daily News*), accepted her poetry and invited her to join their staff as the assistant to the editor of the English section. Once in New York, her life took a dramatically different turn. She interviewed a Socialist millionaire named J.G. Phelps Stokes, fell in love with him, and in 1905 married him. The marriage was performed by Mr. Stokes's younger brother, a rector of St. Paul's Episcopal Church in New Haven.

This fact did not go unnoticed in the Jewish community. One prominent rabbi, Dr. Henry Pereira Mendes, voiced public disapproval while Rose's mother declared: "I am a Jew but I approve of this marriage. I am proud of Mr. Stokes."[14] Some traditional Jewish leaders argued that Rose Pastor Stokes was no longer an acceptable speaker for their groups because she had married outside the faith. The *American Israelite*, however, said in an editorial:

> If Jewish organizations believe that Mrs. Stokes has a message to give them which they could get nowhere else, or which would be of service to them in helping solve certain problems, her marriage outside the Jewish faith should not stand in the way of allowing her to present that message.[15]

Rose Pastor Stokes, a devoted Yiddishist, surely was aware of the disapproval of her coreligionists, but by this time Socialism had become her religion; she probably shared her husband's views when he told reporters: "Neither religion as preached today contains the entire truth."[16] Stokes believed that Jews were particularly suited to the new Socialist religion and she herself was willing to give up Judaism for the new universal religion.

Although she became a key propagandist for Socialism, she remained interested in and involved with Jewish culture. In 1914, she and Helena Frank published a translation of Morris Rosenfeld's Yiddish poems. *Songs of Labor* contained Rosenfeld's poignant descriptions of poor workers trudging to the factory before dawn. His sympathetic and effective portrayals of working-class life, of course, fit into Stokes's scheme. Immigrant Jewish workers were a major constituency for Socialist propaganda: as Jews and workers, they were doubly discriminated against. Stokes spoke to Jewish audiences reminding them of their prophetic heritage and of the relevance of Socialism to their lives in industrial America. Her identification with Judaism was on a cultural, not a religious level. She had rejected Jewish ritual as inappropriate to the new order and as reminiscent of Czarist Russia.

Stokes's career in Socialism continued until World War I broke out, at which time she and her husband split with the Socialist Party of America because of its antiwar stand. Stokes argued that the

Kaiser's Germany was an evil that needed to be destroyed. She supported President Woodrow Wilson's crusade to "make the world
safe for democracy." However, in early 1918, Stokes rejoined the
Socialist Party and spoke out against the war, arguing that the
capitalists profited from the war and not the lovers of democracy.
Her speeches were considered seditious, and she was indicted and
convicted. A federal appeals court overruled her sentence and the
case was dismissed in 1921.

The Bolshevik Revolution split the American Socialist movement;
the loyal followers of Lenin created the Communist Party of America
while the Socialists remained independent of Moscow. Stokes
became a founding member of the Communist Party. In 1923, she
was arrested for attending the 1922 Communist Party convention.
Throughout the 1920s she participated in Communist-led labor
demonstrations. Her return to the Socialist Party in 1918 and her
subsequent alliance with the Communists alienated her from her
more moderate Socialist husband. They were divorced in 1925, at
which time Rose Pastor Stokes scandalized New York readers by in-
forming a reporter that she believed in free love. "Love is always
justified, even when short-lived, even when mistaken, because during its existence it enlarges and ennobles the natures of the men and
women experiencing the love."[17] In 1930, it was discovered that she
had cancer. She died in Frankfurt am Main in 1933 at the age of
fifty-four. Her religious commitment to Socialism never waned.

Perhaps the most exciting and important Jewish woman rebel of
the first thirty years of this century was Emma Goldman. Although
the recent interest in women's history has resulted in a renaissance
of interest in Goldman's life and writings, none of her biographers or
commentators has given comprehensive treatment to her Jewish
origins and the relationship of her Judaic background to her style,
philosophy, and actions. Biographer Richard Drinnon has tersely
described the unique blending of elements that produced Emma
Goldman's anarchism:

> She was a daughter of the rich ethical demands of the prophetic
> strain in Judaism, a product of brutal Russian anti-Semitism, a
> graduate of the radical milieu in St. Petersburg, and a disillusioned
> observer of the gap between ideality and reality in the United
> States.[18]

Another biographer, Alix Shulman, put it this way:

Emma Goldman was born with four curses. She was born Russian, Jewish, female, and unloved.[19]

Drinnon acknowledged the Judaic influence upon Goldman in two areas: her training in prophetic Judaism and her experience as a Jew in anti-Semitic Russia. These two factors, one positive and one negative, aptly summarize the exciting but frustrating dialectic that absorbed many Jewish thinkers and rebels. Their tradition reminded them constantly of the need to bring social harmony and justice to their society while the Christian community in which they lived persecuted them for being Jews. They lived with unjust treatment while studying a history and a tradition that preached social justice. If the positive aspects of the Jewish tradition lost their hold on them, the constant negative force of anti-Semitism reminded them of their identity.

Emma Goldman's autocratic father did not create a compassionate home for Jewish religious observance; though she retained a respect and a commitment to prophetic Judaism, Goldman rejected its formal practice as seen in her father's house. His violent temper, coupled with the slaps of Hebrew teachers, helped give her a negative view of authority, including religious authority. In 1882, she and a sister joined an older sister in Rochester, New York, where Emma Goldman quickly discovered that America's streets were not paved with gold. She worked in a factory and found working conditions appalling. In February 1887, she married a fellow worker named Jacob Kershner in a religious ceremony conducted by a rabbi. Jacob Kershner was impotent and the marriage was dissolved by the same rabbi. A while later, because Kershner threatened suicide, Goldman remarried him. When she decided to move to New York City in 1889, she left him for the last time. The censure of the Jewish community of Rochester surely contributed to her leaving:

I was immediately ostracized by the whole Jewish population of Rochester. I could not pass on the street without being held up to scorn. My parents forbade me their house, and again it was only Helena who stood by me. Out of her meagre income she even paid my fare to New York.[20]

In subsequent years, the intellectually curious Emma Goldman read Socialist tracts, anarchist pamphlets, and the daily newspapers. Anarchist editor Johann Most, the execution of the

Haymarket Square radicals in 1887, and the depression of 1893 radicalized her; in 1893, she gave a speech in the streets of New York telling starving people that they had a right to steal bread if necessary. She was arrested and imprisoned for a year for this speech. Her association with Alexander Berkman, a fellow anarchist who attempted to assassinate Henry Clay Frick, the chairman of Carnegie Steel, earned her the reputation as a terrorist and a dangerous person. "Red Emma" became her label. Rather than letting this deter her, she increased her speaking tours in the early 1900s and crossed the country many times lecturing on anarchism, modern drama, and women's rights. From 1906 to 1917 she and Berkman edited *Mother Earth*, a magazine that expressed her philosophy of life and contained many examples of Goldman's reliance on Jewish history and Old Testament references as essential aids in communicating her message of anarchism to the world.

In her travel report of May 1907, for example, she related a speech she gave in Chicago. Some University of Chicago professors heard her and someone naively suggested that Emma Goldman be invited to speak at the illustrious University of Chicago. But, as she noted,

> they forgot the "principle" for the sake of which the good professor could not invite the Anarchist, E.G. to the College. Probably he thought that at the sound of Anarchism the University buildings would crumble to pieces, as the walls of Jericho did at the sound of the Jewish trumpet. No one can blame the professor—"principle" before freedom of knowledge.[21]

The pages of *Mother Earth* frequently contained translations of a Morris Rosenfeld poem, a Yiddish story, or a tale from the Talmud. Sometimes, in her "Observations and Comments" column, Emma Goldman related a story and then provided an anarchist moral to it, very much in the fashion of a Biblical story followed by a rabbinic interpretation.

> Bocaccio tells it better, but this is it: A Jew, in the middle ages, became a convert to Christianity after a visit to Rome to see the Pope and the cardinals. A wondering friend asked him how he could become a Christian after witnessing the profligacy and corruption at Rome: "Ah," said the Jew, "if Christianity can endure with what I have witnessed, it must hold the truth within it."

The anarchistic moral of the story is that the people would be very happy and very good without government since they can be even as they are under such unspeakably awful conditions as, according to the testimony of expert witnesses, prevail in all departments of the state. [21]

The Yiddish stories translated for *Mother Earth's* readers usually depicted poor workers or the unemployed trying to survive under stressful conditions. "The Child Question," in the February 1907 issue, set the scene tersely:

In the room it was New York, and as cold as it was outside, for in the room lived a workingman, a Jewish pants-maker; and from every corner bitter, killing Want looked out, for the pants-maker was on strike.[23]

The child's continual questions could not be answered by the tearful mother, who waited patiently for her husband to return hoping that he had found work. The story ended sadly:

The child fell asleep with the piece of bread in her hand. And the striker's wife wept silently.[24]

To Emma Goldman, the Jewish worker's plight could not be solved by Judaism; nor could it be resolved by capitalism or Socialism. Anarchism, she argued, was the only salvation. Human beings had to be freed of all external shackles in order to fulfill their own individuality. Judaism, Christianity, the state, and the legal system were all bonds, chains of enslavement, that had to be removed for human freedom to be achieved.

To connect with her audience, however, and to utilize the rich tradition and experience she knew, she frequently related examples of social injustice to Jewish experience. The plight of the American black did not escape Goldman's notice. In one discussion of "the situation in America," she noted:

The persecution, suffering and injustice to which this much-hated race is being constantly subjected can be compared only to the brutal treatment of the Jews in Russia.[25]

Immigrant Jews in America, survivors of Czarist persecution and anti-Semitic pogroms, were uniquely qualified to understand and empathize with the plight of the black Americans. To Emma Goldman, the Jews as victims should identify with all of the victims of Christian societies.

Emma Goldman's faith in anarchism did not make her forget her Jewish identity or the particular burden Jews faced in a hostile world. She frequently spoke and wrote about anti-Semitism as a living enemy. In an "Observations and Comments" column of September 1908, she noted a recent newspaper report in which General Bingham, New York's police commissioner, claimed that the majority of New York's criminals were Jewish. Bingham, she continued,

> never could learn to handle the truth as carefully as he does his revolver. Prison statistics indisputably prove that the percentage of Jewish criminals is practically a negligible quantity. In the New York penal institutions the Jews are by far in the minority, proportionately and absolutely. But the Commissioner, large-souled soldier that he is, never did care for such trivial things as facts. . . .

> In the face of accumulating proofs that the majority of New York criminals are in the Police Department, the chief thief-catcher cries "Crucify the Jews!" It is necessary to distract public attention from the multiplying charges of inefficiency and corruption. Fortunately, New Yorkers know Bingham too well to take him seriously. Otherwise he might be crowned an American Krushevan.

Goldman, in a footnote, told her readers that Krushevan was a Russian professional Jew-baiter responsible for inciting pogroms against the Jews.[26]

Goldman's style of writing and speaking also displayed her Judaic heritage. Not only was her content frequently sprinkled with Biblical references and Yiddish stories, but her narrative style resembled that of a Biblical storyteller as well. In an essay called "Defying the Gods," Goldman began:

> That the Lord is a spiteful old gentleman everybody knows. He is never more content that when he can make his children feel his Almighty power. As to the unfortunate ones born of

Lucifer,—such as the Anarchists, for instance,—no punishment is ever adequate to their crime. To deal with them God has created a special tribe, the uniformed species of man.[27]

Goldman's rhetoric adapted the Biblical framework for modern purposes. Combined with her well-developed sense of irony, her presentations, both oral and in writing, were powerful. Goldman received well-deserved praise as an orator and though policemen dogged her lecture trail, constantly harassed her, and tried to prevent her from speaking, she traversed the country every year for about twenty-five years and spoke in both small towns and large cities. In 1910, for example, her six-month lecture tour took her to thirty-seven different cities in twenty-five states; she delivered 120 lectures to a total audience of about 40,000 people.

Butte, Montana; Seattle, Washington; Pittsburgh, Pennsylvania; and Malden, Massachusetts were all visited by Emma Goldman. "In Malden, Mass.," she told her readers,

a dismal looking town, reminding one of the puritannical sterility of papa Endicott's times, the original hall keeper showed the yellow streak. Again the search for a hall. One half-finished was found; with the aid of a few Jewish radical boys, who appropriated the "Shabbess" candles of their mothers, the darkness of Malden was somewhat relieved. The edict of the Chief was, of course, against Anarchy. But who cared?[28]

The image of Jewish boys appropriating their mothers' Sabbath candles to provide light for Goldman's lecture hall is an ironic one. The notion of using the light of tradition to illuminate the new tradition, the new world view, surely appealed to Goldman.

In many large cities with a significant Jewish population, Goldman held separate meetings in Yiddish for the Jews. The first Yiddish lecture in Los Angeles was given by Goldman in 1910. Cleveland, she reported in one summary of her travels, was always a "faithful friend."

The crowning effect in Cleveland, though, was the Jewish meeting. Though the latter was arranged by only one comrade, and for a Monday, a large crowd received me with the usual intense Semitic warmth, which always makes the Trail less difficult.[29]

In Chicago in 1912, she said:

> The Jewish meetings proved most interesting. Apart of being the
> largest, they were also the most worthwhile, because of their
> quality. Certainly no other race will furnish from five hundred to
> a thousand people interested in such subjects as "Art and Revolu-
> tion" or "Chantecleer," nor will one easily find so much
> understanding and fine appreciation among other people.[30]

Her 1912 visit to the University of Wisconsin at Madison yielded
disappointing results:

> MADISON is still on the map, but the students don't make it a par-
> ticular credit to the rest of the world. There are exceptions, of
> course. The average student, however, could learn much from
> some of our Jewish shop girls and boys. The latter are by far more
> alert, interested and intelligent, than these pampered American
> fellows, to whom college life is but a means to more successfully
> meet the world of greed and power.[31]

And on Sioux City, Iowa, she wrote:

> The most pleasant experience of my visit in Sioux City was the
> meeting of the group of Jewish men and women, mostly Socialists,
> who are carrying on effective educational work through the
> Hebrew Progressive Library. They have a beautiful little hall of
> their own, with quite a variety of books, and the members are
> most eager to read and learn.[32]

Goldman's lecture topics were wide ranging. She was an expert
on modern European drama, an early advocate of birth-control information for women, and a scintillating speaker on anarchism. Her
English was amazingly good, both spoken and written; she was a
zealous reader as evidenced by her wide references and her fine
vocabulary. During the 1910s, one of the subjects that got her into
the most trouble was birth control. She went to jail in 1916 in New
York over this issue as it was illegal to discuss the subject publicly.
To Goldman, women were an especially oppressed group. They were
tyrannized by their fathers and husbands, exploited in the market
place, and chained to a Judeo-Christian tradition that considered

them child breeders. In a 1908 short story called "At Twenty-Six,"
Goldman criticized the Judaic view of women:

> Yankel's mother died when he was four years old and she was
> twenty-six. There were two others, younger than he. She died of
> galloping consumption.
>
> What should a father do, who is left so? Marry again; what else?
> Marry a housekeeper who will claim no wages, a faithful nurse
> who will serve his children. As to the woman, well—what of her?
> Can he afford to consider her? . . . And for what is a woman born?
> For what does a man thank God that he is not so born? . . .
>
> Being a Jew, he married his dead wife's brother's child; and at
> eighteen she was thrust into this loveless life of serving
> and—bearing. Ten children were the fruitage of her body,—"as
> many as God gave."[33]

The question "For what does a man thank God that he is not so
born?" referred to the morning blessing recited by the observant
Jewish man. Contemporary Jewish feminists also point to this prayer
as evidence of Judaism's male chauvinism. Emma Goldman noted
this unjust reference early in the century. She once recalled that her
father said that girls did not need very much education: "Girls don't
have to learn much . . . only . . . how to prepare minced fish, cut
noodles fine, and give the man plenty of children."[34]

Goldman displayed a real familiarity with Jewish prayers, ritual
observances, and holiday practices. Her particular criticism of
Judaism was based on firsthand knowledge of her religion, but it
also fit into her larger schematic critique of all religions and all ar-
bitrary systems.

Goldman was critical of the women's suffrage movement, believ-
ing that it did not reach for the goals of a humanistic-anarchistic
world. Suffragists merely imitated men and the material values of
bourgeois society. She lectured that women should strive for full
human development, free of all strictures. A woman's independence,
she argued, had to

> come from and through herself. First, by asserting herself as a
> personality and not as a sex commodity. Second, by refusing the

right to anyone over her body; by refusing to bear children, unless she wants them; by refusing to be a servant to God, the state, society, the husband, the family, etc.[35]

Within Goldman's philosophical framework, all people needed to liberate themselves from all formal bonds that controlled their thoughts and their lives, but women especially needed retraining in freedom, a state with which they were wholly unfamiliar.

Emma Goldman's career was abruptly halted by the United States government in 1917 when she was sent to prison for opposing the draft. Two years later, upon her release, she was deported as an undesirable alien to Russia. Emma Goldman and her lover, Alexander Berkman, both exiled, found the new Bolshevik Russia unsympathetic to anarchists; they became the first major critics of Lenin's new order and for this they were excoriated by Marxists all over the world. Goldman left Russia, and lived in France, Canada, and England during the remaining twenty years of her life. She briefly visited America in the 1930s but never again had the audience she had so enjoyed during the first two decades of this century.

Emma Goldman personified the complete rebel, the rejector of all systems. To a true anarchist like herself, no religion, no government, no force could or should harness human development. Judaism, like all "isms" except anarchism, had to be rejected within this context. But Emma Goldman's roots, her spirit, and her approach to the world were firmly planted in Jewish soil. She especially hoped that the Jews—God's Chosen People, as she ironically reminded her Jewish audiences—would see the light and embrace anarchism. She enjoyed sharing her ideas on Ibsen and modern drama with her Jewish audiences. They were her "comrades," even those who did not agree with her ideologically.

According to historian Melech Epstein, there were more radicals among the Jewish immigrants of the 1904–1914 decade than in the previous twenty years.[36] Many of the young men and women who came to the United States had experienced the 1903 pogroms of Kishineff and Bessarabia, the 1905 Russian Revolution, and lived with the knowledge of the Bialystok and Byelorussian pogroms of 1906.

Among the arrivals were thousands of young men and women who had been active in underground revolutionary work in their home towns, had fought in the *selbstshutz* (defense units) against the pogroms, had seen the inside of Czarist prisons or been exiled to

Siberia. Transplanted also was quite a sizable intelligentsia of all political groupings.[37]

Among the politically aware population were many Socialist women willing to participate in labor struggles, union organization, and propaganda efforts. The garment manufacturers became the American counterpart of the Czar. The exploitation on Henry Street and the tyranny of St. Petersburg were pieces of the same cloth. When the Bolshevik Revolution occurred, the *Jewish Daily Forwards* ran headlines such as: "*Mazel Tov* [Congratulations] to our Jewish people; *Mazel Tov* to the Entire World."[38]

During the 1920s, the Jewish Communists infiltrated many of the locals of the International Ladies Garment Workers Union. They had selected the women's garment workers because, as Epstein notes, they were likely

> to be the most receptive audience because of their known militancy. But, as their (the Communists') experience with trade unions was practically nil, their appeals outdid in dogmatism those of their party.[39]

The Communists were eventually routed from the affiliates of the International Ladies Garment Workers Union and the Amalgamated Clothing Workers; but during the 1920s, Communists participated in the activities of the union.

Jewish women often worked as organizers for the Jewish section of the Communist Party and as spokeswomen for the Party's views within their unions. Rose Wortis of the dressmakers' union became a leader in the Communist Trade Union Educational League. Miriam Zam, a member of the Young Communist League in the early 1920s, worked with her husband Herbert in the League in Chicago.

> ... Miriam, also a devoted Communist, had to give up her college and turn over the money her parents sent her for tuition to feed the few people in the league office and pay the return fare of League delegates.[40]

The Communist wife, like the bourgeois wife, became the self-sacrificer. Her goals, her professional advancement, her wishes had to be subsumed under those of her husband, the Party, and the "comrades." The absence of women's names among the leaders of the Communist Party bears witness to the chauvinism of the Party.

A loyal minority of Jewish Communists, male and female, never abandoned their original faith to radical change. But as external conditions tested that loyalty—the anti-Semitic trials in Russia during the 1930s, the Nazi-Soviet pact of 1939—some gave up Communism for New Deal Democratic politics or American-brand socialism. The Jewish working class was diminishing in number as the immigrant generation grew older and their children moved into white-collar positions, the business world, and the professions. The radicalism born in the sweatshops of New York and Chicago disappeared with factory-inspection laws, better economic conditions, and the aging process.

The two key personalities described in this chapter, Rose Pastor Stokes and Emma Goldman, were unique products of the Jewish and American cultures; they came of age as expanding capitalism displayed its ugliest features. Their personal encounter with Judaism was more negative than positive: autocratic fathers, repressive communities, and fanatical observances that seemed irrelevant to modern living. Both women, intellectually curious, ambitious, and excited about living in a new country in a new century, sought to devise a personal philosophy that explained industrial evils and social institutions while providing personally satisfying values for living. Stokes found such a synthesis in the new socialism-Communism of the period; Goldman rejected all social systems and opted for an individualistic creed that placed responsibility for human growth on each individual.

They shared many beliefs. Both viewed the marriage institution as a restraint upon female expression and growth; both believed that Judaism and Christianity favored men over women and tolerated the double sexual standard. Both rejected religious rituals as means of keeping human beings in obeisance to an antiquated tradition. Their fundamental difference of opinion centered upon how the perfect society would be attained: Goldman argued that only anarchism could create truly human exploration and fulfillment, while Stokes asserted that a socialist system was the only basis for a just society. As each woman searched for new ways to mold the humane community, she traveled farther and farther away from her origins. Indeed, they both saw that departure as essential for their own personal growth as well as for society's progress. But Emma Goldman, more so than Rose Pastor Stokes, never forgot her Judaic heritage and never lost her admiration for the Jewish people's ability to survive all adversities.

4. Volunteer Activists: The First Two Generations

The immigrant Jewish women garment workers spent some of their brief hours of leisure organizing and planning philanthropic functions for their needy sisters and brothers. However, among the middle and upper classes of native American Jewish women, more time could be spent in volunteer charitable activities. By the 1880's, most of the Jewish women of Sephardic and German descent enjoyed a comfortable existence. According to one study based upon the 1890 census, forty percent of the German Jews in New York had at least one servant and ten percent had three or more.[1] The husbands and fathers of these women were generally of the merchant and manufacturing classes and the women were the beneficiaries of their success. Their numbers were small relative to the thousands of immigrants newly arriving from Eastern Europe after 1880, but they used their economic and social power to establish Jewish institutions that affected the new immigrants as well as all subsequent generations of American Jews.

Fraternal organizations, synagogues, Jewish hospitals, and B'nai Brith chapters already existed among American Jewry by the late nineteenth century. And Jewish women acted as volunteer workers in the synagogues and hospitals in the Jewish community. But none of these organizations could deal effectively with the immigrants' needs; none was geared toward aiding the new arrivals in finding a place to live and to work. In the prevailing mood of the time it was assumed that all individuals would help themselves; no public monies were spent aiding the unemployed, training the deprived, or encouraging the education of poor children. American Jews knew that if they did not help their fellow Jews, no one else would. The mammoth task of staffing the philanthropic organizations created by the Jewish community fell upon the able shoulders of Jewish women.

Performing good works, after all, was a natural extension of women's work, and economically privileged Jewish women were well suited to such activity.

As one magazine writer noted in 1927: "[Jewish women] are more active than ever in philanthropic service—a natural sphere for the mother-instinct of the sex."[2] Many of these prosperous women had extensive experience administering their large households and could readily transfer their skills to charitable work. Ambitious, competent Jewish women could not, given the cultural imperatives within which they lived, rebel against their society and become lawyers in great numbers. Everyone expected them to marry, raise a nice Jewish family, and perpetuate their culture. Most middle- and upper-class Jewish women conformed to this set of expectations. But when given the opportunity to act beyond their home in philanthropic endeavors or synagogual activities, many grasped the opportunity offered them. They rightly interpreted their good works as mutually beneficial; they personally grew and utilized their native talents for organization, leadership, and administration while serving their fellow Jews. Further, this activity harmonized with their social role of wife and mother. There was no role conflict; nurturing and caring for the underprivileged was, after all, woman's traditional work. Society positively approved of their generous support of the immigrants. Further, synagogue activities and Jewish cultural activities were also viewed as proper extensions of the role of the Jewish wife.

Both the *shtetl* experience of Europe and the religious commitment to preserve their organic community ensured the creation of Jewish philanthropic and social-service structures. By the late nineteenth century, each city with a large Jewish population boasted a hospital, fraternal organizations, orphanages, and senior citizens' homes. Middle- and upper-class Jewish women, by virtue of their position in the community, were expected to be the fund raisers, often the volunteer teachers, and the cultural sponsors. The Jewish men decided how to spend the money raised by the women.

Many of the first generation of women who became volunteer activists devoted a lifetime to public philanthropy and Jewish social service. As the organizations they worked for changed, so did they, adapting and altering their contributions depending upon the changing needs. Many of the volunteer activists to be described in these pages became major interpreters and analysts of the whole social-service enterprise. Many observed, with some trepidation, how the volunteer worker was shunted away in favor of the new "professional"; some tried to adapt to the new organizational structure while others retired from public activity.

Volunteers have never received their due in the Jewish or American culture. Most often, "volunteer" has meant female, free labor, and such labor has gone unrewarded. This is true of Christian and secular humanitarian volunteers as well as Jewish volunteers. Few historians adequately document and credit women's volunteer work in churches, hospitals, orphanages, and settlement houses. Historians of Jewish communal life, for example, refer only in casual and brief terms to the role Jewish women played in the synagogue and philanthropic organizations. One account of Los Angeles Jewry noted in passing that "cultural activity was a woman's responsibility,"[3] while another recent historian acknowledged the women's role though he offered no detailed discussion of it:

> . . . the story of the synagogues of the United States gives clear testimony that the survival of Judaism has been enormously helped, perhaps even made possible, by the dedication, the devotion, the directed energy of American Jewish women. Only very recently has their contribution been acknowledged. The recognition is, as yet, by no means adequate; too often it is grudgingly given.[4]

The basis for the grudging recognition is worthy of a study in itself, but the general omission of women's contribution to the social, cultural, religious, and humanizing efforts of Judaism in historical accounts requires correction. Historians have often grouped together all forms of volunteer activity—cultural, social, and philanthropic—into one indiscriminate whole when in fact the nature of each form of volunteerism is different from that of the other. A synagogue fund-raising event, for example, serves a social and pragmatic purpose while a lecture by a visiting scholar satisfies intellectual and cultural needs. Each is important, but the two are not interchangeable or identical. Jewish women acted as volunteer workers for synagogues, local charitable groups, regional chapters, and national Jewish welfare organizations. They responded to the multiple needs of the Jewish community at multiple levels of organization.

Often, the most involved Jewish volunteer activists were middle-aged women who became "organization" women after their children were grown or at least were all in school. Their husbands usually supported their work and often actively encouraged it. Jacob Schiff directed his wife and daughter's philanthropic activities carefully. Henry Solomon, Hannah Solomon's husband, admired his wife's work with the National Council of Jewish Women, an organization she founded. Indeed, it was often the financial success of the husband that contributed in two different ways to their wives' becoming volunteer activists: first, by providing enough money to relieve the wives of domestic duties, and second by contributing to their wives' causes. A husband's support was essential as these women often became full-time workers for their organizations and spent many hours and days away from their homes and families. Without their husbands' support, both financial and psychical, most women volunteers could not have done their good work, and many women gratefully acknowledged the role played by their husbands.

Besides married women with families, many volunteer activists were single women who spent time in volunteer activities before marriage or, if they remained unmarried, throughout their adult lives. They devoted themselves to their cause with a single-mindedness that was impressive. Henrietta Szold is probably the most extraordinary example of this type of woman. Some women, such as Esther Loeb Kohn, were widows; in Kohn's case, she was financially well-off, childless, and aching to perform good works. Living in Chicago at the turn of the century, she found enough worthwhile causes to occupy her for a long lifetime, which is precisely how she spent her years from 1909 to 1965.

Jewish women, of course, had already experienced the joys and frustrations of synagogual and communal work before the arrival of the new immigrants. And this work, perpetuating the Jewish community in America, continued to be performed, and still continues to be performed, by Jewish women in their communities all over the United States. But two new concerns emerged with the enormous growth of the Jewish population: social service for the immigrants and the appeal of Zionism. The first, most compelling problem to be confronted was: How do you absorb the thousands and tens of thousands of Russian Jews arriving at Ellis Island every year? Where do you house them? How do you help them gain employment, shed their old European ways, and become Americans? The male leadership of the New York Jewish community (New York, of course, was the destination point for the overwhelming majority of immigrants) answered this question reluctantly at first, and then with greater urgency as the need increased.

They established specific agencies, such as the Hebrew Immigrant Aid Society (HIAS), to help the new arrivals. No one agency seemed able to handle the enormous task. In Chicago, Hannah Solomon worked with the Chicago Women's Club and Hull House but decided that a separate organization was needed as well. In 1896, she founded the Bureau of Personal Service. Jewish women became the administrators and the daily workers of the newly created organizations. However, even with the impressive response of the Jewish community, most arriving immigrants, especially after 1900, received aid from relatives rather than an agency. Further, many immigrants proudly sacrificed some security rather than accept financial help.

Zionism came to America as well with the new immigrants. The idea of a Jewish homeland as the only safe haven for persecuted Jews appealed to the exiled Russians. It took American Jews a few generations to respond to this new ideology; indeed, many American Jews did not become sympathetic to the Zionist philosophy until the World War II period and the destruction of six million European Jews. But in the first years of Zionism's appearance in this country, from the 1890s to the World War I period, a number of important Jewish women became active propagandists for Zionism; one woman, Henrietta Szold, founded Hadassah, the Zionist World Organization's women's group; she became the most effective spokeswoman for a restored Zion in the world. At the turn of the century, she was preceded by Rosa Sonneschein and Mary Fels, who spoke and wrote about the need for a Jewish homeland. Sonneschein, in fact, was one of three Americans, and the only woman, present at the first World Zionist Congress in 1897 in Switzerland. In the magazine she edited, The American Jewess, she sang the praises of Zionism.

Communal work, immigrant social service, and Zionism, then, became three demanding, difficult, and time-consuming areas of work for Jewish women volunteers. And the women responded to the pressing needs unpretentiously and uncomplainingly. Most of them are not known or remembered; their names may appear on local lists but most of the written records have been discarded. Except as a memento, no one keeps the program from last year's synagogue dinner dance. Similarly, the women who did not have leadership positions in social-service or Zionist work are also forgotten, but their work and their accomplishments remain a living testimony to their contributions. The following discussion of some of the leaders must represent the anonymous thousands of volunteers as well.

To most of the leaders among the volunteer-activist women, their mission was clear: to ease the suffering of their fellow Jews. They yearned to do "practical good," as Hannah Solomon said; that was their role as Jews and as women. Their religious commitment formed the essential base for their good works while the social role of women provided the respectable opportunity to nurture, to heal, and to aid the sick, the orphan, the poor, and the delinquent. Like all good Americans, they sought the best available solution to an immediate social problem. At the opening of a National Council of Jewish Women meeting, or at a conference of the National Federation of Temple Sisterhoods or a Hadassah function, the words of the Old Testament or some contemporary rabbi were heard. The Jewish context of these women's work was never forgotten. Judaism played an integral role in their philanthropic activities; they understood the meaning of *tzdakah*, of righteousness as the motivation for good works.

The volunteer activists of the 1890s and all subsequent generations were extremely talented women. They learned quickly, dealt with people ably, understood the virtues of efficiency, and adapted to changing circumstances. Hannah Solomon recounted how good record keeping was essential when her Bureau of Personal Service was distributing relief funds to neighborhood people. She learned about the frustrations of overlapping services and worked to streamline her organization. Many of the volunteers, though they remained volunteer workers for many years, truly became professionals in their work, experts in their field. Sometimes their community recognized this fact and rewarded them with an honorary degree or community award.

The tension between the volunteers and professionals that emerged in the social-service agencies and the settlement houses represented a conflict between generations, classes, and outlooks. The upper-class, German Jewish women volunteers looked down upon the aspiring middle-class professional, who was often a generation younger. The women volunteers, experienced in the day-to-day work of the organization, lacked the academic training respected by, and demanded of, the new social workers, especially in the post–World War I era. At the turn of the century the volunteers dominated; eventually, however, they would lose out in the relentless push toward professionalization.

Jewish communities in Chicago, New York, Philadelphia, and smaller communities met the challenge of the new immigrants by creating agencies to deal with each specific need. In Chicago, for example, in 1893, a Home for Jewish Orphans and a Home for Aged Jews were both established. The sisterhoods of New York City's Reform synagogues contributed money, material aid, and time to the new immigrants; they formed day nurseries, kindergartens, clubs, and classes through the auspices of the United Hebrew Charities. In Philadelphia, the Esrath Nishim ("Helping Women"), an old organization founded in 1873, reconstituted itself as the Jewish Maternity Association and started a hospital known as the Maternity Home. Ladies Auxiliaries in Philadelphia also visited the poor and provided clothing and services to the newly arriving poor immigrants.[5]

The organizing structure was usually the same in each city: the sisterhood, ladies' auxiliary of a synagogue, or a separate woman's group was founded to deal with a concrete social problem. In Los Angeles, where the numbers were much smaller, women leaders of the established Jewish community opened the Educational Alliance in 1911 to provide for the immigrant. The Young Women's Hebrew Association was also founded in the 1910s.[6] Indeed, by 1918, each community with a substantial Jewish population had developed a vast number of social-service organizations. The Jewish Communal Register reported 3,637 organizations for New York City. "That meant one organization for every 410 Jews."[7]

One reason for the proliferation of organizations in each city was the fact that the Russian Jews created their own structures as soon as they could. In Chicago, for example, the Orthodox Jews would not use the hospitals, the orphanages, and the old people's homes established by the German Jews for fear that these institutions did not observe the dietary laws and the Sabbath. So Chicago Orthodox Jewry established Maimonides (later Mount Sinai) Hospital rather than use the German Michael Reese Hospital; they created their own old-age home, orphanage, and sheltering home.[8] German Jews continued to utilize Michael Reese Hospital, as did less observant Russian Jews. In all cases, however, Jewish women became the major volunteers, the foot soldiers who implemented the policies established by the male boards of directors. The women staffed the agencies, administered relief, and counseled the needy.

Much of the Jewish idealism that survived in the new world we owe to the woman and she in turn received her inspiration from the National Council of Jewish Women, founded through the efforts of the indefatigable Mrs. Hannah G. Solomon.[9]

Philip P. Bregstone, the author of the above quotation, considered the creation of a national Jewish women's organization a major breakthrough for Jewish women.

> While the Jewish woman enjoyed greater freedom in affairs of the home, her general status was even more circumscribed than that of her non-Jewish sister. She was given no part in the religious affairs of her people although the education of her children was under her exclusive supervision. She had no voice in the social or political life which belonged to the domain of man. He was master of the household, legislator and administrator. It was only his love for his family, his strong affection for her and their children that made her condition tolerable.[10]

The National Council of Jewish Women (NCJW) enabled the Jewish woman to leave the house respectably, to make important decisions, and to raise her self-esteem. Hannah Solomon told her own story of the founding of the NCJW in her autobiography, *Fabric of My Life*. In 1890, she had been approached by Mrs. Potter Palmer and Mrs. Charles Henrotin, two prominent Chicago women whom Solomon knew through the Chicago Women's Club (Solomon and her sister were the first Jewish members of that club in 1876), to organize a Jewish women's section for the upcoming World's Columbian Exposition. Palmer and Henrotin were in charge of the Women's Exhibit. Solomon agreed that as part of the Parliament of Religions, a major feature of the World's Fair, Jewish women should be represented.

> But how could I go about it; how reach the right women? Not only were there no organization lists available . . . there was not even a federal organization![11]

She decided to write to rabbis all over the country. In all, she wrote ninety personal letters, "all by hand," as she noted.[12] In 1892 Solomon was so encouraged by the response to the Jewish Women's Congress that she resolved that this meeting would be the beginning of a permanent national organization. Henrietta Szold, Josephine Lazarus, and Minnie D. Louis, all able and well-known women, spoke at the 1893 Congress and supported a national Jewish women's organization. Louis, a New York educator of Jewish immigrants, ended her remarks to the Congress with:

You Jewish women of Chicago, all Israel honors you! You have in-augurated a new mission of enlightenment! Like unto Samuel, you have gathered us together to unite us, that we may gain strength, to arouse in us a thirst for better knowledge of our people and our trust, with a more loyal allegiance to both, through which we may become invested with that holiness that will make even our enemies worship us.[13]

The spirit of Judaism permeated all of the meetings, and in the final session ninety-three women representing twenty-nine cities, resolved to meet regularly and call their organization the National Council of Jewish Women.

Resolved, that the National Council of Jewish Women shall (1) seek to unite in closer relation women interested in the work of Religion, Philanthropy and Education and shall consider practical means of solving problems in these fields; shall (2) organize and encourage the study of the underlying principles of Judaism; the history, literature and customs of the Jews, and their bearing on their own and the world's history; shall (3) apply knowledge gained in this study to the improvement of the Sabbath Schools, and in the work of social reform; shall (4) secure the interest and aid of influential persons, wherever and whenever and against whomever shown, and in finding means to prevent such persecu-tions.[14]

The first stated purpose of the NCJW aptly highlights the Jewish, the womanly, and the American dimensions of the founders. "Religion, Philanthropy, and Education" are integral concerns of Jewish women while the search for "practical means of solving problems in these fields" is particularly characteristic of American pragmatism. For every problem there is an appropriate solution. Good works, in both the Jewish and Christian sense, become the mode to achieve the desired solution.

Through her work with the Chicago Woman's Club, Hannah Solomon had participated in the creation of an emergency workroom for needy women during the depression of 1893-1894. She decided that such an activity was also appropriate for the NCJW. In 1896-1897 she founded the Bureau of Personal Service, a clear-inghouse agency to deal with the multiple needs of the Russian Jewish immigrants in the seventh ward of Chicago, where most of them lived. The Bureau, which Solomon chaired from its inception until 1910 when it was absorbed by the Associated Jewish Charities, investigated financial needs of immigrants for the Woman's Loan Society, studied tenement conditions for industrial reports, directed parents with troubled children to the proper agencies, and cooperated regularly with the settlement houses in the area such as Hull House and its Jewish counterpart, the Maxwell Street Settlement House.

The Chicago chapter of the NCJW also established a Sabbath school for girls, as the traditional Talmud Torahs did not provide for young women. Three hundred girls signed up immediately and the demand was so great that Sinai Congregation, a large Reform Jewish temple on the South Side of the city, took over the operation. NCJW members visited delinquent children who had been sent to prisons in every city where they had a chapter. In Chicago and New York, for example, the NCJW women were largely responsible for the establishment of a separate juvenile court; Minnie Low, Solomon's superintendent of the Bureau of Personal Service, became an unpaid probation officer of the court as did her aide, Minnie Jacobs Berlin.[15] In New York, Sophie G. Axman, who worked with the Educational Alliance, an organization established by German Jews for the immigrants, became the chief parole officer of the board of justices of the court of special sessions. All of these women began as interested volunteers and became expert in the field of judicial procedures and juvenile delinquency.[16]

As the social-reform activities of Solomon expanded, she realized the need for predictable and efficient methods of organization. "It must be remembered," she recalled,

> that when the Bureau was opened, there were few trained social service workers, even among the superintendents, and nearly all women assistants were volunteers. There was little scientific administration of charities and practically no collaboration among the different agencies. Our methods of administration were entirely inadequate; a fact I realized even at that time, and expressed thus, in my first Bureau report: "We can no more run charities on the old lines than a business house can chalk the names of its customers on the barn door."[17]

Because Solomon's husband Henry was a successful businessman and her family was prominent in Jewish and civic affairs, she remained content to be a volunteer activist all of her long life, never accepting financial remuneration for her work. Indeed, the idea of a salary did not occur to women of her class. They viewed social service, particularly Jewish social service, as a religious obligation as well as a class privilege.

> My husband's interest and cooperation in everything that I undertook was of greatest importance to me. In fact, without his constant encouragement, I could not have continued, satisfactorily, on my way. He was my chief advisor and many a time his ready financial assistance eased the way. Often, when problems arose, he aided in their solution, buoying up my flagging spirits, sharing in my every endeavor with quick understanding and wisest counsel.[18]

Solomon was an effective administrator and leader. She enjoyed coordinating the various activities sponsored by the NCJW. In 1895, she participated in the creation of the first Conference of Jewish Women. Twenty-six groups joined together "for the purpose of specializing the charity work of these organizations, to prevent duplication in the distribution of relief."[19] This effort was the first of its kind in the country for Jewish women's groups, and, in many cities, the first attempt to solidify all charitable organizations. In the case of Chicago, it was not until 1900 that the Associated Jewish Charities was formed in an attempt to centralize all of the city's philanthropic organizations. Each city went through a similar process; first proliferation of many specific groups to meet specific problems followed by a consolidation and coordination of charitable efforts so as to avoid duplication and overlapping functions. It is important to note the important lead that Jewish women's organizations took in this process.

Within the NCJW there were both Orthodox and Reform Jewish women. Solomon, a follower of Reform, discovered opposition to her leadership at the 1896 convention when some Orthodox women questioned her position as leader since she did not consecrate the Sabbath in the Orthodox manner. Solomon answered her critics with: "I consecrate every day of the week!"—a statement that "was hailed with touching acclaim, and [she] was duly re-elected."[20] When Solomon returned home, she found a floral piece, prepared by her husband and three children, which read: "I consecrate every day." Solomon's daughter Helen followed in her mother's footsteps and led the first Jewish day nursery. Solomon's sister Henriette, her sisters-in-law, and her cousin Lizzie Barbe helped her in the various activities of the NCJW as well as in the organizational aspects of coordinating conferences of Jewish women. When the Associated Jewish Charities was formed in Chicago, Solomon became the only woman board member, representing the women's societies on the board. In 1905, she refused to be reelected president of the NCJW and devoted herself to board activities in Chicago as well as the Park Ridge School for Girls, a particular interest of hers.

From 1893 to 1905, while Solomon was leading the NCJW and administering its programs in Chicago, the New York City chapter developed many similar programs. Although all national organizations establish an agenda, each local chapter picked and chose the projects of the national platform that interested it the most. The New York group met single immigrant women at the docks and helped them get settled. They provided a shelter, the Clara De Hirsch Home, until more permanent arrangements could be made. They also visited Jewish women in jail, contributed monies to Jewish orphans, and established a workroom for women.[21] The activists of the New York chapter often received publicity, as they were located in the city with the heaviest concentration of immigrants and their work was the most visible.

Rebekah Kohut, a founding member of the NCJW and a New Yorker, spoke for the organization widely. The young widow of a prominent rabbi, Kohut became a well-known speaker for Jewish causes. In 1900, she founded the Kohut School for Girls with her stepson George and with the financial aid of Jacob Schiff, noted Jewish philanthropist. She spoke for women's suffrage as well as for religious suffrage for Jewish women. Kohut believed that Jewish women should be given equal treatment in the synagogue. She commented on the Orthodox practice of seating women and men in separate sections in the synagogue:

> My participation in America in many campaigns for women suffrage had made of me a self-conscious champion of equal rights. In being obliged to mount the gallery where the women sat by themselves behind curtains shutting them away from the eyes of the males below, I underwent an internal rebellion. I thought one ought to pray alongside those with whom one is united by family ties.[22]

It is interesting to note the interconnections between the campaign for women's suffrage and the crusade for equal rights in Judaism. Solomon, a friend of Jane Addams, often spoke for women's suffrage as a natural extension of women's rights. Like the women's rights movement of the 1840s, early twentieth century Jewish women who worked for the cause of others, gained self-confidence and asserted the need for their own rights as well. Abbey Kelley, a famous abolitionist, became a feminist while working for the freedom of slaves; Jewish women doing communal work for the immigrants came to appreciate the need for women's suffrage. They also looked more critically at the synagogue, a male domain, and wondered why they could not sit side by side with their husbands, be counted in the daily prayer service, and preach from the pulpit. Solomon, in fact, became the first Jewish woman to preach at Dr. Emil G. Hirsch's Sinai Congregation in Chicago in 1897.

Jewish women, then, active in volunteer Jewish philanthropic organizations, broke the stereotype concerning the proper role and behavior of Jewish women. When Rebekah Kohut began speaking for the NCJW in the 1890s, she said that public speaking was regarded as revolutionary behavior

> because, no matter what Gentiles did, Jewish women were expected to stay at home and occupy themselves with housekeeping, sewing bees, card playing and tea parties. To have opinions and to voice them was not regarded as good form even in the home. But to have opinions and to speak them out in public meeting! One would have to belong to my generation to understand.[23]

Kohut, raised by a father who believed that his daughters should "face the world 'like men',' " resented the pampered treatment given many young women.

> Oh, the tragedy of this petty, human pride that renders young women useless for anything but to sit behind a silver service, dispensing tea and small talk! Bringing up the future mothers of men with no knowledge except "social graces."[24]

Kohut's world view did not reject, or neglect, the important role of wife and mother for all Jewish women, but she interpreted the characteristics of that role far more broadly than traditionalists allowed. Jewish women could, and should, contribute to society, use their brains for a variety of constructive purposes, and raise their children to be thinking people; this required, according to Rebekah

Kohut, better education and greater social opportunities than were usually accorded Jewish women.

While the charitable activities of the NCJW received approval from most observers, the organization did not go uncriticized. Rosa Sonneschein, the wife of a Reform rabbi, lived in Chicago during the 1890s and, from 1895 to 1899, edited and published a magazine called *The American Jewess*. In it, she reviewed the activities of individual Jewish women as well as groups such as the NCJW. She had an interest in religious suffrage for Jewish women and wrote regularly about the need to admit single Jewish women to membership in congregations. When Temple Isaiah in Chicago did so, Rosa Sonneschein took credit for the action and called upon the NCJW to influence other congregations to do likewise. Temple Isaiah's president was Henry Greenebaum, Hannah Solomon's uncle.[25]

But by 1896, Sonneschein had her doubts about the direction that the NCJW was taking. In an essay called "The National Council of Jewish Women and our Dream of Nationality," she argued that the reason why the NCJW had only 3,000 members was not because Jewish women were not smart enough or interested enough in social change, but because the NCJW did not have an ideal sufficient to excite Jewish womanhood.

> It is deplorable that at the inception of the organization no central idea was generated, and it's almost incomprehensible that two years of its duration have elapsed without developing any specific object.[26]

To Rosa Sonneschein, the idea that could generate excitement among American Jewish women was Zionism.

> The time may be upon us in which it will be possible to restore Palestine to the Jews, to restore our nationality; which does not mean that the Jews who are patriots of the land in which they are born should leave their country and flock to Palestine, but that we may have a religious center, and re-establish the home of our ancestry for those Jews who are driven from country to country by race hatred and religious persecution. There is abundant Jewish money in the world, and enough Jewish influence among the Powers of Europe, to make this ideal feasible.[27]

Sonneschein foresaw greater respect for Jews in all countries of the world if a Jewish Palestine existed; she believed that all peoples would respect the Jews and tolerate them if they had their own national state.

"The work may seem gigantic and out of woman's sphere; but at present it's woman who has the time, the inclination and the faculty to pursue great objects."[28] Hannah Solomon and the NCJW did not agree with Rosa Sonneschein. They believed that there were more than enough social-service projects within their own communities with which to deal; as good Americans, they were suspicious of any nationalist idea that detracted from their commitment to America. Hannah Solomon confessed in her autobiography that

> Zionism has never seemed more than the despairing cry of a forlorn hope and I still believe that Palestine is destined to be a buffer state in which nothing can, or will, count to other nations but its usefulness to them.[29]

Solomon visited Palestine in 1923 and came back even more convinced of the inefficacy of a prospective Jewish state, though she hoped that the persecuted Jews of Europe would always find a haven there.[30]

Rosa Sonneschein found little support for her Zionist ideas among Reform Jews, but she received a more sympathetic response when she discussed the need for Judaism to modernize in the area of the roles of women.

> As a rule a Jewess is content to leave to her husband and sons the wisdom of election and selection for political office. Her aim is for social and religious equality, with the privilege to become individually and collectively a factor for common good.

> Blind obedience to prescribed laws, ancient and modern, made all Jewish women religious automats, that move and follow closely the lines directed by man. Here, as in many other walks of life, men make the laws and women obey them. At present medieval decrees annulled by reform have left her in a barren religious sphere. She has blabbered the Hebrew prayers without understanding a word of them, adhered to commands never explained to her, and followed a routine of harassing precepts transmitted with sublime ignorance from dame to daughter.[31]

In another essay, Sonneschein referred to the "despotism" of Jewish men as inappropriate behavior in modern America.[32] Reform Jewish temples allowed both sexes to sit together during prayer services and provided Sunday School classes for Jewish girls and boys, but these measures were not sufficient. Sonneschein envisioned a religious environment in which total equality prevailed. The principles of the Declaration of Independence blended with those of the Torah, she believed, and Jewish practices had to be updated.

In the summer of 1897 she attended the first World Zionist Congress, the only woman among the three Americans present. Her report in the October 1897 issue of *The American Jewess* showed her continued commitment to women's rights in Judaism as an essential principle:

> And strange to say, with this strong craving for liberty and equality, the Zionists began their proceedings by disfranchising women. I am sorry that I have to relate this fact, as the subject is Oriental, but not Jewish. . . .
>
> The Oriental Jew naturally shared some of the customs reigning supreme in the land of his adoption. And at the same rate as the Jews drifted away from Mosaic Judaism, those customs became rabbinical laws. And so it happens that some delegates attending the Congress came from provinces still adhering to those antiquated laws relating to women. It was feared by the leaders of the Congress that it might disturb the feeling of that element if women would be admitted to vote. It was undoubtedly policy that dictated that step, but it remains to be seen whether it was wise policy. We therefore reserve the right to dwell at some future time, with more leisure, on this subject, which is of vital interest to the women of Israel.[33]

In her report on the second annual Zionist Congress in 1898, she noted that the New York Zionists elected Mrs. Richard Gottheil as a delegate, and thus the Congress had to take cognizance of women's presence. Sonneschein's minority voice was silenced in 1899 when, because of ill health, she stopped publishing *The American Jewess*.

Sonneschein and Solomon, both living in Chicago in the late 1890s, represented contrasting points of view about the role of Jewish women in America. Both agreed on the need for public lives for Jewish women, though they differed on the nature of those lives. Both applauded Reform Judaism's inclusion of women as respectable and equal members of the congregation and both viewed the

Jewish woman as an essential pillar in community work. Hannah Solomon typified the American pragmatic reformer and Rosa Sonneschein exemplified the visionary idealist. Solomon shared, with her Protestant acquaintances, a commitment to good works. She believed that, once given aid and training, the immigrants would assimilate into the American mainstream. They would become productive Jewish Americans whose children would exhibit the same virtues as all middle-class Americans. Sonneschein's ambitions were on a grander scale. She expected Jewish American women to work for a homeland that they might never visit and for fellow Jews they did not know.

Mary Fels, the widow of soap manufacturer Joseph Fels (Fels-Naptha Soap], also became an advocate of Zionism during the 1910s. Joseph Fels, who died in 1914, had devoted many years to Henry George's single-tax cause. He believed that private land that was not being used should be taxed; most importantly, the single tax would eliminate exploitation of the land and of workers. Owners would not receive excessive profits from unearned income.

Fels continued to publicize her husband's single-tax proposals. She advocated them in *The Public*, a magazine she coedited with four others from mid-1917 to March 1919[34] and combined this work with her espousal of Zionism. In a January 4, 1918 editorial entitled "Rebuilding Palestine," she suggested that Palestine had a golden opportunity to build itself upon sound human and economic principles:

> Here lies the opportunity for the Jew to demonstrate a great truth to the world by uniting the Mosaic principle of land ownership with a just system of taxation.[35]

Land should be taxed, she argued, but not the improvements upon it. In this way, labor values would not be taxed, landowners would not receive undue gains, and land speculation would be stopped.

Fels saw her devotion to Palestine and to her late husband as being interwoven:

> It was to this cause that Joseph Fels dedicated himself and his fortune; and had his life been spared he would today be banding all his energies toward aiding the Zionists in rebuilding Palestine on a solid foundation.[36]

Besides her writings and speeches on behalf of Zionism and the single tax, Mary Fels donated over one-and-a-half million dollars of her personal fortune to Palestine. The 1917 Balfour Declaration encouraged her and all Zionists to believe that Great Britain and all the Western powers would aid in the establishment of a Jewish national home. Although the dream of a Jewish homeland did not materialize until after World War II and the destruction of six million Jews had occurred, Mrs. Fels lived to witness the creation of the State of Israel. She died in 1953 at the age of ninety.

Henrietta Szold's contributions to Palestine stand in a category all by itself. Even before she became a full-time activist for Palestine, Henrietta Szold had demonstrated her exceptional talents in two other constructive areas: her first career as teacher and educational administrator began with her graduation from Western Female High School in Baltimore in 1877 and lasted until 1893; for sixteen years she taught at the Misses Adams School and from 1889 to 1893 she organized and ran a night school for Russian Jewish immigrants. A typical day in Szold's life during this period went like this: she rose at 5:30, began writing instructional letters to her teachers at 6:30, breakfasted, went to the Misses Adams School where she stayed until 3:00, ordered some materials for her night school, attended a Botany Club meeting until 6:00, ate supper, and at 7:00 went to the Russian school until 11:30.[37]

Henrietta Szold's second career, which lasted twenty-three years, was as secretary of the editorial board of the Jewish Publication Society (JPS), a position she held from 1893 to 1916. She demonstrated her erudition, her tact, her administrative efficiency, and her editorial skill in this important job. The scholarly writings of the JPS became an invaluable contribution to Jewish knowledge and Szold's editorial talent left an indelible mark on all of the JPS publications. The yearly edition of the *American Jewish Yearbook* was one of her regular publications. She moved to New York with her mother in 1903 (her father, Rabbi Benjamin Szold had died the previous year), continued her editorial work with the JPS and became the first woman student at the Jewish Theological Seminary. Szold became part of a women's study group in New York and wrote articles on Judaism and Zionism for various publications. She gave her first public speech advocating a Jewish homeland before a local chapter of the NCJW in January 1896.[38]

Henrietta Szold went to Palestine for the first time in 1909. She returned to this country enthusiastic about the possibilities of building a homeland. In February 1910, she became secretary of the Jewish Agricultural Experiment Station in Palestine, an organization headed by Julius Rosenwald and supported by Rosenwald, Nathan Straus, and Julius Mack, all of whom became her good friends and respected colleagues. Thus, while continuing her work with the JPS, she established her first organizational tie to Palestine. On Purim, 1912, she founded the Jewish women's Zionist organization, Hadassah, a Hebrew word for "myrtle," the name of Queen Esther. Hadassah had two primary purposes: to propagate the cause of Zionism in the United States and to establish visiting nurses in Jerusalem. The woefully inadequate medical facilities in Palestine stood out in Henrietta Szold's mind as the most pressing problem needing correction.

Szold combined absolute conviction with compassionate respect for disbelievers in Zionism. In a letter to Rosenwald's wife, Augusta Rosenwald on January 17, 1915, she diplomatically tried to engage the philanthropist's aid, knowing full well that Mrs. Rosenwald was not a Zionist:

> If you succeed, in your appeal to the Federation of Temple Sisterhoods, in conveying to the Jewish women of America the need of such a sanctuary for the Jew, the need of a center from which Jewish culture and inspiration will flow, and if you can persuade them to set aside one day of the year as a Palestine Day, on which thoughts and means are to be consecrated to a great Jewish world-organizing purpose, you will have accomplished a result that will bring immediate blessing to those now in distress and in terror of life. . . .[39]

Her numerous personal letters (she was an inveterate letter writer) contained both her warmth and her total devotion to Zionism. The recipient could not help but be impressed with the writer's energy and commitment.

In 1916, through the generous financial support of Judge Julius Mack, Henrietta Szold became financially independent and able to resign from her full-time job with the JPS. Now she could begin her third career in earnest. At fifty-six, Henrietta Szold became a full-time propagandist for Palestine and a vigorous booster of Hadassah, which became the world's largest Zionist organization in her lifetime. After World War I, the Zionist Organization of America reorganized and she became the head of its Education and Propaganda Department. In 1920, she went to Palestine as the American representative on the Executive Committee of the Medical Unit for Palestine. Except for a three-year stay in New York (1923-1926), she remained in Palestine until her death in 1945. She learned conversational Hebrew [she already knew biblical Hebrew and was very well educated in traditional Jewish texts), began visiting all of the medical facilities throughout the country, and amazed all observers with her vigor, her patience, her kindness, and her command of all administrative details.

Henrietta Szold displayed the spectacular blending of the Jewish tradition, the Progressive commitment to social change, and the application of Jewish leadership principles in a woman. Although her public persona was always that of a modest, retiring woman, she took great pride in her work and only delegated authority when she was assured that her successors would do a good job. After establishing her night school in Baltimore, she stepped aside and let the city of Baltimore administer it.[40] She shared the American belief in practical solutions to social problems as well as the optimistic commitment to the idea that positive change could be effected. Her work in education and Jewish scholarship were important activities in and of themselves; but they also became the substantial foundation for her life's work: providing medical facilities through Hadassah's fundraising efforts for Israel.

Throughout her life, Szold added responsibilities upon her shoulders; indeed, as she grew older, she became more and more active. In 1927, she was elected one of the three members of the Palestine Executive Committee of the World Zionist Organization, the only woman on the committee. She was in charge of health and education for the whole land. During the 1920s, in fact, when Zionism was in a weak organizational position, Hadassah increased its members to 27,000.[41] Irma Lindheim, the American President of Hadassah at the time, credited Henrietta Szold with that amazing accomplishment. "She reduced the general Zionist idea to a particular part of its program and then proceeded to develop bit by bit the instrument with which to construct this part."[42]

Joan Dash's recent biography of Henrietta Szold, *Summoned to Jerusalem*, described the intricate infighting that characterized the Zionist Organization of America throughout the 1920s. Leader Louis Lipsky was an enemy of Hadassah, an organization he believed was led by feminist women. In 1928 he accused Irma Lindheim of being a feminist and having abandoned the spirit of Henrietta Szold:

What was formerly a Jewish woman's movement—auxiliary, complementary, aiding and comforting the main stem of the movement—became an organization animated by the sense of women's rights. Like all other women's movements of this sort, it represented resistance to the domination of men, which resistance was turned into a demand for equality which, as soon as it was attained, became a desire to dominate and control.[43]

Lipsky wanted control of the finances of financially healthy Hadassah and he was willing to accuse the Hadassah leaders of being women's rights advocates, the worst label one could assign to traditional Jewish women. By 1933, Hadassah won the right to preserve its autonomy within the Zionist organization.

Henrietta Szold's public appearance as a modest, respectful woman may have fooled some of her contemporaries, but those who knew her all agreed that she had a steely interior, a deep resolve, and great willingness to remain committed to a cause she believed in. She identified with the Louis Brandeis wing of the American Zionist movement, a group that shared her belief in pragmatic, gradual change, in careful negotiation, and in rapprochement with the opposition. Szold tried to avoid open confrontation among Hadassah, the American Zionist Organization, and the Palestinian branch of the organization. However, she faced many obstacles. The European wing of the Zionist movement and the Jews and Arabs in Palestine brought different perspectives, passionate leaders, and complex rivalries to the difficult subject of Zionism.

Throughout her life in Palestine, Henrietta Szold preached for a binational state, a land that equally respected Arab and Jewish rights. "Differences," she once said, "do not make civilization; but differentiation does."[44] She criticized Zionist colleagues who disregarded the rights of the Arabs; and she questioned the British unwillingness to deal with terrorists. In a letter home in 1921 she noted:

> Palestine is an empty land. The Jew need not and will not rob the handful of Arabs of their rights or their property. Palestine could be made a land of immigration for the Jews if the Christian and Moslem agitators were not thinking of their own advantage.[45]

As she grew older, her strength, patience, and concern for others remained vital and alive. "I find that, old as I am," she wrote in 1934, "in a certain sense I haven't stopped growing. While I don't understand, while my intellect is an organ of narrow limitations, my inner world—perhaps it is my world of feeling, or instinct—expands."[46] She always remained a traditional Jew and once insisted, diplomatically of course, that the British governor of Palestine, Sir Ronald Storrs, serve her a kosher lunch.

When the Nazi menace appeared in the 1930s, Henrietta Szold, along with her European colleagues, organized Youth Aliyah, an organization devoted to removing Jewish youth from anti-Semitic Europe. She has been personally credited with bringing 8,000 children out of Germany. Szold greeted the new arrivals at the docks of Haifa, kept track of their progress in the new land, and visited with them regularly. In fact, she continued to travel all over the country throughout the 1930s despite great personal hardship, poor transportation conditions, danger from hostile Arabs, and advancing age. She continued to coordinate all of the medical facilities in the land, the social services, and Youth Aliyah until her death, at the age of eighty-four, in 1945.

Henrietta Szold combined the practical good-works orientation of Hannah Solomon and the idealism of Rosa Sonneschein. Indeed, it was this brilliant synthesis that enabled Hadassah to become, in 1980, the largest Jewish women's organization in the United States. As will be discussed in the next chapter, the NCJW, though still in existence, did not grow as much as Hadassah because its specific social needs were accomplished. Szold's Hadassah resembled other middle-class women's organizations in structure, but its attachment to Palestine and then Israel elevated it in significance. Zionism was a cause, a goal; after the creation of the State of Israel, its overwhelming need only increased Hadassah's obligations.

Henrietta Szold's basic approach to a problem followed that of her fellow Progressives. She isolated it, concretized it, and shaped a solution to it. Once she focused upon Zionism, an ideal goal, she translated the goal into realizable units. She decided, for example, that medical facilities should be her primary concern and so she concentrated upon that aspect of building Palestine. When she witnessed the rise of Nazism, she devised Youth Aliyah. Her constant letters to America, her fund-raising trips, and her close communication with her supporters kept her tied to her financial source. The Hadassah membership always knew what was happening in Palestine thanks to Henrietta Szold's letters. While American and world Zionism faltered in numbers, Hadassah kept growing. Jewish women identified with Henrietta Szold's cause; they enthusiastically followed her leadership; and they found their good works on behalf of Palestine compatible with their role of Jewish wife and mother. In an essay on education written when she was twenty-seven, Henrietta Szold wrote:

> Everywhere can be discerned prognostics of the fact that life in the twentieth century will not be easy to live, that it will call for high courage to face the truth, steadiness in action, steadfast opinions and unflinching purposes.[47]

Henrietta Szold met the twentieth century's challenge and displayed the steadfastness and the courage necessary to live in this century.

The second generation of Jewish women volunteer activists came of age in the 1920s. Many joined the already established Jewish women's organizations such as Hadassah and the NCJW. Pearl Franklin, for example, joined Chicago's Hadassah chapter in 1921 and within a year became its local president. During her tenure in office, the membership increased from 300 to 3,000. Another important women's organization, Women's American ORT, expanded its membership. In 1933, Chicago Jewish women began their first ORT chapter in that city. ORT, the Organization for Rehabilitation through Training (founded in 1880), concentrated on fund raising for vocational schools for Jewish youth in various parts of the world. Jewish women, of course, continued their work in local synagogue sisterhoods, in the women's auxiliaries of the *landsmanshaften*, and in the Jewish hospitals, orphanages, and community centers.

In communities with very few Jews, the Jewish women became volunteer activists in the general women's clubs and rose to positions of leadership. Julia Bloom Mayer of Iowa City, for example, was president of the Iowa Federation of Women's Clubs in the 1930s and the director of Des Moines' Jewish Community Center which was, according to the governor of the state, "one of the outstanding social institutions of the city. Non-sectarian in everything but name, the Center offers every sort of social and intellectual stimulus to the people of the community."[48] Mayer retained her Jewish identity while serving the whole community.

The second generation of women volunteer activists also found themselves ministering to new needs. In San Francisco, in 1920, the Jewish community formed the Jewish Committee for Personal Service in State Institutions. The function of the committee was to visit Jewish patients in mental hospitals and to provide psychiatric social services. The historian of the committee's work noted that "no other religious or ethnic group attempted a like program, nor did the state itself."[49] Elsie Shirpser became the assistant executive secretary of the committee in 1925 and its executive secretary in 1929. She remained in that position for twenty-four years. Shirpser successfully lobbied for a state mental health survey.[50]

Jewish organization women of the second generation attended national meetings of the recently formed (1914) National Federation of Temple Sisterhoods (NFTS). By 1928, over 300 temples were represented with the national organization boasting a membership of 55,000. In a special 1928 issue of *The American Hebrew* honoring the sisterhoods, the editor wrote:

> Although the activities of these respective sisterhoods center around their synagogues, they foster also many worthwhile local causes which would otherwise languish. . . . In a sense, the leadership of these women is needed to insure the very preservation of Jewish religion and culture.[51]

Temple sisterhoods raised the needed funds for synagogual activities, served as volunteers in the religious schools, and supported all religious and cultural events held in the temples.

Mrs. J. Walter Freiberg, president of the NFTS in 1928, spoke before the convention and emphasized the adult-education component of the NFTS's program. "My message to all Jewish women," she said, "is to know your religion, develop a Jewish consciousness and make it an integral part of your daily life."[52] The format of the NFTS mirrored that of many religious and secular organizations of the period. With the growth of cities, the middle class, and improved communications during the Progressive Era, Americans incorporated businesses and civic groups into national networks. The NFTS's yearly conventions resembled that of Hadassah, the NCJW as well as the National Council of Negro Women and the General Federation of Women's Clubs.

By the second generation, a new social type of Jewish woman was emerging: the professional board member. Middle- and upper-class Jewish women, who devoted a lifetime to Jewish organizational work, engaged in a new social role. They joined one or more groups early in their married life, worked as a volunteer, participated in committees, and eventually assumed leadership positions in the organization. Chicagoan Esther Loëb Kohn is an example of this new social type. In 1909, Kohn was widowed at the young age of thirty-four. As a member of a prominent German Jewish family, she was financially comfortable and eager to live usefully. Her late husband had had a special interest in medical care for schoolchildren and Kohn decided to pursue social work as an extension of his work.[53] In 1911 she moved to Hull House, an unusual step for a wealthy Jewish widow.

Kohn's neighborhood volunteer projects acquainted her with the social and working conditions of Chicago's immigrant Jewish children. She witnessed ten-year-old children making paper flowers until midnight only to fall asleep at their school desks the next morning. Kohn decided to lobby for a child-labor law in the Illinois legislature. Her knowledge, experience, and spirited presence made her a familiar figure in both Springfield and Chicago and resulted in her membership on multiple boards and committees associated with the child-labor issue. Kohn's position as a professional board member on both secular and Jewish boards lasted for forty years.[54]

While working for the end to child labor, Kohn served on the Michael Reese Hospital board, and as director, vice-president, and president of the Jewish Social Service Bureau of Jewish Charities from 1921 to 1941. In the 1930s she worked for the Jewish refugees in Nazi Germany and provided financial aid to those who succeeded in coming to the United States. She enlisted the financial support of other prominent Chicago Jews such as Julius Rosenwald for all of the Jewish social-welfare agencies.

She was both a witness to and a commentator on the transition in social-service agencies from entirely volunteer workers to professional staff. When Hull House experienced leadership problems after the death of Jane Addams, Kohn spoke for creating a structure where both volunteers and professionals shared in decision making.

> Because of the wealth and variety of knowledge which a resident volunteer group has to offer the House, I think Hull House should follow modern trends of agency organization and have at least joint staff committees of staff and volunteer residents in formulating policies. This is a democratic method of organization and a method which secures the best service for the money spent. . . .[55]

In another context, while arguing that trained lay people should assist the medical staff to perform social services in a hospital, she noted that lay persons expressed

> the community's interest in social progress. The professional social worker came into being largely because lay men and women recognized a need for a more scientific approach to social problems and set about to develop the resources and training which would bring this about. Professional social work could hardly have achieved its present state without their material help and support.[56]

Kohn's lifetime devotion as a volunteer activist became a model for three generations of women. She never tired of reminding her audiences of the value and importance of volunteer work. Esther Loeb Kohn's work, in both the secular and the Jewish community, was greatly appreciated by her contemporaries. Although a strikingly beautiful and extremely bright person, she preferred to shun the public eye. She only gave public speeches when prevailed upon. In 1960, Esther Loeb Kohn was named the "Sweetest Woman of the Year" and, more significantly, awarded the Golden Age Hall of Fame Award from the Jewish Community Centers of Chicago.[57] Like Hannah Solomon, Henrietta Szold, Mary Fels, and the other women described above, Esther Loeb Kohn became an expert in social service. She knew, from firsthand observation, what poverty and need meant and she learned to work through legislatures, committees, national organizations, and wealthy friends to obtain the desired social goal. Kohn died in 1965 at the age of ninety.

In 1937, the Business Women's Council was formed in New York City in order to gain the financial support of business and professional Jewish women in New York and Brooklyn. This occasion signified the recognition on the part of the male-run Jewish Federation that there were a significant number of Jewish businesswomen who were potential contributors to Jewish causes independent of their husbands. The Council became part of the Women's Division of the Jewish Federation. Among the organizers were Ann Goodman for the specialty-shop fields, Dr. Alice Bernheim for the women physicians, and Helena Rubenstein for the cosmetics field.[58]

By the 1930s, Jewish community services had become so elaborate and expensive that fund raising became the primary activity of Jewish women volunteers. Direct participation in the life of the immigrant community was no longer necessary, nor did professionals welcome volunteers in their domain. Jewish women interested in volunteerism found Hadassah to be a useful and rewarding organization and the cultural and education programs of the NCJW stimulating. Self-development and fund raising for medical facilities in Palestine became the foci of these women's organizations, a major shift from the social-participatory role played by the earlier generation of Jewish women volunteers. Jewish women with leadership ambitions found the exclusively women's organizations more congenial to their aims than the male-dominated Federation boards. Women sat on an occasional board and administered their own women's Division board, but men controlled all of the Federation boards throughout the country. A few women such as Hannah Solomon and Esther Loeb Kohn sat on Federation boards, but they were the exception rather than the rule.

Esther Loeb Kohn had envisioned a situation in which volunteers and professionals worked compatibly in Jewish social-service agencies. The unique experience of voluntarism, she believed, should never be lost to the community nor should the volunteers be denied self-fulfillment. Unfortunately, Kohn's hopes have not been entirely realized. The role of women volunteers in the daily administering and operating of most social-service agencies has been eliminated, though the roles of fund raiser and programmer are still being performed.

5. Volunteer Activists: 1945–1980

This is a true story: In the 1970s, a young Christian woman converted to Judaism in order to satisfy the religious requirements of her Jewish boyfriend. She completed the religious-instruction program, went to the *mikvah* (ritual bathhouse), and married her Jewish fiancè. Two years later, at a Friday night dinner at her in-laws' house, she mentioned casually that she had just joined Hadassah. Her mother-in-law became ecstatic: "Now you are a Jew!" she exclaimed.

To many contemporary Jewish women, Jewish identity is determined by communal organizational ties to Judaism. One recent source has noted that forty-five percent of all American Jewish women belong to a Jewish women's organization, as compared to thirty percent for all American women.[1] De Tocqueville commented on how Americans were a nation of joiners; American Jewish women fit into that behavioral pattern with enthusiasm. They belong to their synagogue's sisterhood, their local chapter of Hadassah, Women's American ORT, and the Women's Division of the Jewish Federation. Some add other special-interest Jewish organizations as well as a plethora of "general American" organizations to this list.

In recent years, roughly the same proportion of Jewish American women belong to synagogues and to Jewish women's organizations.[2] None of the Jewish women's organizations insists upon a particular brand of Judaism. Conservative Jewish women (40.5 percent of the households) and Reform Jewish women (thirty percent) belong to many of the same organizations.[3] Orthodox Jewish women (six percent of the households) often join the Mizrachi Women's Organization of America rather than Hadassah or ORT. The National Council of Jewish Women, based upon informal inquiries, seems to draw its membership largely from middle- and upper-class Reform Jewish women.

Becoming a member of a Jewish communal organization is a popular form of Jewish identification, for men and women alike. Attending cultural meetings; raising money for Israel, a major new role since 1948; and learning about Jewish history and literature appeals to the one-and-a-half million members of Jewish women's organizations. In this way, the women demonstrate a positive commitment to their Judaic heritage though not necessarily a religiously observant devotion to Judaism. This may be a second- and third-generational response in that at least among the first generation the rationale for Jewish women's participation was not to find a substitute for religiosity but rather another essential component in the commitment to an organic Jewish community. Hannah Solomon believed she "consecrated every day" when she worked for the Jewish immigrants, but her social work did not replace attendance at the temple. Similarly, Henrietta Szold observed the holidays, the dietary laws, and all Jewish rituals while supervising medical units in Palestine.

Religious education for Jewish women has been limited at best. As a result, since the 1920s adult Jewish American women have used their organizations as adult-education agencies to learn about Judaism, religious practices, Jewish history, and, since 1948, the State of Israel. Indeed, the overwhelming adult interest in Jewish education is easily evident to any reader of a Hadassah bulletin or a schedule of ORT lectures. Although fundraising remains a primary function of all Jewish women's organizations, so is Jewish education.

This is a phenomenon characteristic of second-, third-, and fourth-generation American Jews. In the early 1900s, the Jewish woman immigrant had to adjust to the new realities in America while retaining the religious practices she brought with her from Europe. Her daughters learned Jewish cooking and holiday observances in the home while growing up. Most likely, her granddaughter and great-granddaughter learned about Judaism from a Jewish woman's organization. The formal religious education of a Jewish girl did not include holiday preparations; ideally, young Jewish girls, aged eight to thirteen, studied Hebrew and Jewish history in English in both Reform and Conservative schools, but few learned their lessons well or continued their religious education beyond thirteen—just like most Jewish boys. The Jewish woman of the third and fourth generations, then, grew up learning less within her household about the woman's role in preparing holiday celebrations and still less in religious schools about her heritage.

The leadership of the Jewish women's organizations as well as the male-led Federation boards appreciate the fact that an informed and enthusiastic membership is a more supportive membership. Sophisticated knowledge about fund-raising techniques, including the introduction of the "plus-giving" tactic, has made the middle- and upper-class Jewish woman the target of many organizational drives. Jewish women are working in large numbers and have independent incomes, thus making them contributors separate from their husbands. Psychologists inform professional fund raisers that participatory members are more likely to become contributors than passive followers. Further, the social status of attending a $500 luncheon sponsored by the Women's Division of the Jewish Federation is not lost on many socially conscious women. Thus, in addition to the idealistic and authentic interest in education, Jewish women join Jewish women's organizations for sociability, knowledge of their Jewish past and present, and the moral satisfaction they derive from knowing that their contribution and participation are preserving Judaism. These, of course, are no mean goals.

In 1910, Hannah Solomon founded the Conference of Jewish Women's Organizations to provide a coordinating mechanism for the plethora of Jewish women's organizations in each city. By 1950, in Chicago alone, 186 organizations were members of the Conference. One hundred thirty-nine were clubs, forty-five were local sisterhoods, and two were affiliates of national or state organizations. While some of these groups supported a particular orphanage or old-age home, others were social groups that were parts of *landsmanshaften*. Still others were women's divisions of men's organizations. The following is a list of the top eleven (in membership) Jewish women's groups in Chicago in 1950.[4]

Name	Membership	Founded
Hadassah Sr., Chicago Chapter	13,500	1912
B'nai B'rith, Chicago Women's Council	12,000	1938
Women's Division, Jewish Federation of Chicago	6,500	1934
National Council of Jewish Women, Chicago Section	3,000	1893
Women's American ORT, Chicago Region	3,000	1945
American Jewish Congress, Chicago Women's Division	2,500	1937
Daughters of Zion Infant Home & Day Nursery	2,500	1914
Jennie Rubenstein Memorial Assoc.	2,000	1938

Jewish People's Convalescent Home	2,000	1933
Mizrachi Women's Organization, Chicago Council	2,000	1924
Pioneer Women	2,000	1925

The Women's Division of the Jewish Federation, organized in the 1930's, recognized the importance of women's groups for fund-raising projects. Further, as one contemporary participant and reporter on Jewish women's groups noted in a 1948 essay:

> The Women's Division, therefore, was organized to interpret the work of the Jewish Charities to all the women of the community, to coordinate the activities of women's groups in meeting the problems of the Jewish community, to educate women on social welfare needs, and to develop leadership through Jewish community work.[5]

New York City and all other cities with significant Jewish populations followed the same path. With the growth of Nazism in the 1930s, the American Jewish community tried to raise funds to aid European Jewry while maintaining all of their social services for American Jews.

In 1946, the Women's Division of the United Jewish Appeal (UJA) was created as a separate fund-raising instrument for overseas relief. This organization has been described in a recent article as a "plus-giving" device.

> That is, the general campaign solicits the husband as the "head of the household," with the prestige and status accompanying the contribution accorded to him. The Women's Division provides the woman with the opportunity to make a gift of her own right—from her salary if she is working outside the home, from her personal household funds, or from funds directly under her control.[6]

The UJA is the superstructure devoted to fund raising for Israel in the United States. Its separate Women's Division raised about fifteen percent of its total funds in 1975.[7] In Chicago in 1976, the Women's Division of the Jewish Federation (which funds and supervises all social services as well as the UJA Drive) contributed nine percent of the Federation funds. The concept of "plus-giving" is the major rationale for this structure's creation. The following table shows the membership numbers for the top Jewish women's organizations.

Top Ten Jewish Women's Organizations, 1976
(By approximate membership)[8]

Organization	Members
Hadassah	350,000
Women's League for Conservative Judaism	200,000
B'nai Brith Women	150,000
Women's American ORT	115,000
National Federation of Temple Sisterhoods	110,000
National Council of Jewish Women	100,000
Brandeis National Women's Committee	65,000
Mizrachi Women's Organization of America	50,000
Pioneer Women	50,000
Women's Branch of Union of Orthodox Congregations	35,000

Since the middle 1960s, Jewish American women have listened to women's liberation speeches that emphasize the need for a woman to fulfill herself. They have read feminist writings that question volunteerism, laud personal satisfaction, and challenge the family structure. As both leaders and followers in the women's movement, Jewish women have had to come to terms with the meaning and relationship of feminism to Judaism and their personal philosophy of life. Few had questioned the importance of volunteer activities; few had considered their communal work nonpaid, or exploited, labor. The perspective was new, the degree of probing surprising.

As well-educated members of the Jewish American community, women were sensitive to the new message. Those who defended their wifely/motherly/volunteer life found the exploration and the defense to be an energizing, positive experience. Those who accepted the new feminism and rejected the traditional female roles often sought personal rewards in new occupations and professions. Some returned to college to complete a degree, others joined Jewish women's organizations to seek their self-definition through a new association with Judaism, and still others tried to reform religious Judaism to harmonize with the new feminism.

The women's movement of the 1960s and 1970s has required all self-aware women to examine their values, their lives, and their future plans. Self-examination, indeed, has been the hallmark of many recent reform movements. I recently sent a questionnaire to twenty women leaders of Chicago chapters of Hadassah, Women's American ORT, and the National Council of Jewish Women. In it I asked: "What are your feelings about the role of women volunteers?" The following are some selected but typical responses:

If every woman went back to school and/or work, who would do the job of the volunteer?. . . I remember being interviewed by a news reporter and he asked my occupation, and I stated housewife or homemaker. This was about four years ago. If I was to be asked that question again I would say I was a volunteer.

I feel it is an important—really very important—role and often sadly underrated by the volunteers themselves. It is important to the survival of the Jewish community and also important to the survival of the "Jewish" woman. Right now, volunteerism is looking second best to the career opportunities that are now available to women. I don't think it will continue to look second best, as women will begin to see that they will need both the career and volunteer activity in their lives.

The volunteer organization educates, enriches and stimulates the human potential within its participants. There is much gratification in the successful accomplishment of goals and in the growth of Jewish identity in our own lives and its related efforts of the entire community.

The work I do as a volunteer in many areas would not be done, service couldn't be performed, if it has to be paid for. It would be a sad state for the community affairs without the role of the volunteers.

Some Jewish American women are combining families, careers, and voluntarism. The Jewish Federation as well as Hadassah and other Jewish women's organizations hold evening meetings in order to attract the growing numbers of Jewish women careerists. Single women, whose numbers in the traditionally family-oriented Jewish organizations has been slight, play an increasingly large role in the Young Peoples Division of the Jewish Federation as well as Hadassah chapters.

Thanks to the women's movement, the status of the volunteer has been raised. Women volunteers are receiving greater recognition for their efforts. However, feminist rhetoric has sometimes been confusing. While feminists criticized American society for ignoring its women volunteers, women were told to demand salaries for their homemaking work. Capitalism, the profit system, and competition were denigrated by the same feminists who told women that their volunteer work symbolized their low self-image. Were women fools not to demand salaries for their volunteer activities? Were they hiding in community affairs rather than face the competitive job world? Was self-fulfillment synonymous with a profession or job? From the responses given by Jewish women leaders and from the evidence offered by all of the activities of the Jewish women's groups, it would seem that Jewish-organization women have integrated the best of the feminist philosophy and rejected the untenable aspects.

The 1967 Arab-Israeli War, the 1973 Arab oil embargo, and the 1979 fall of the Shah of Iran have also motivated many Jewish women to play more active roles in their organizations. The fear of rising worldwide anti-Semitism has energized Jewish groups to educate everyone to the dangers of prejudice. In the late 1970s,television reported on American Nazi activities and showed the films *Holocaust* and *Playing for Time*; the 1980 presidential election campaign also became an agenda item for all Jewish women's organizations. Knowledge of current events of concern to Jews has become a regular feature of Jewish women's programs.

While feminism has become a public and private concern for most Jewish women, the official leaders of the Jewish women's organizations have been slower to respond. While Hadassah, for example, speaks out strongly against anti-Semitism and stresses the need for continued support for Israel, it was not until February 1977 that Hadassah gave public support to the Equal Rights Amendment. It displayed great hesitancy in taking a stand on a feminist issue. One commentator on the subject of Jewish women and feminism has noted that:

> Although [Jewish women leaders] do express sympathy for certain feminist goals such as equal pay and equal oportunity for

women, the women who have risen to leadership in the Jewish community are not generally sympathetic to the "women's libbers," as they call them.[9]

Other critics have suggested that:

Many active Women's Division members view the Women's Division as a vehicle for feminist expression. Others see the Women's Division as evidence of the rampant sexism of the UJA.[10]

Given the new consciousness, although not always the attendant acceptance, the women's divisions of each Jewish Federation organization have had to consider their position relative to the overall organization. Should they remain separate and equal (unequal), or shoiuld they demand a merger with the Jewish Federation board?

The volunteer bureaucracy of the Jewish Federation and its companion, the UJA, is formidable. Since 1946 there has been a National Women's Division within the UJA structure. In 1962, a National Young Leadership Cabinet was established to recruit and train young leaders. Largely as a result of the heightened interest and awareness of women leaders within the organization, the Executive Committee of the UJA voted in August 1976, by a vote of nine to eight, to include women in the National Young Leadership Cabinet. The arguments against inclusion of women expressed fears that sexuality would charge the already charged atmosphere, women's rights would attain too much prominence,and men would lose their position of authority.[11] Clearly, the very feminist issues that were being debated in the law schools, elementary schools, homes, and businesses of America were also being discussed and debated within the Jewish Federation.

The very fact that the few prominent women in Jewish Federations around the country have spoken publicly about the role of Jewish women in Jewish philanthropy and social services underscores the new concern for this subject. Jacqueline Levine, former President of the Women's Division of the American Jewish Congress and Vice-President of Jewish Federations and Welfare Funds, was one of the highest-placed Jewish women leaders in the Federation superstructure. In a 1972 speech given before the General Assembly of the Council of Jewish Federations and Welfare Funds (the umbrella organization for the more than 200 local Welfare Funds in the country), she described the role of women in the Jewish community. Although hopeful for positive change, she quoted from a study of women's participation on Federation boards done by the Council which showed unimpressive results.[12]

In cities with large Jewish populations, under thirteen percent of the board members were female; the percentage rose slightly in smaller communities. Women were better represented on board committees, but their numbers and percentages remained modest at best. While the survey suggested a new awareness—after all, no one had ever framed such an enquiry before—the results were disappointing, a fact acknowledged by Levine. The organized Jewish community viewed women as wives, a traditional definition, and not as individuals, the new feminist goal.

Jewish American organizations, as Levine's study and most others confirmed, reflected the general sexism of American society. Jewish culture, after all, accepts the general American view that money matters and financial decision making are male concerns. Women's functions and expertise are restricted to women's fund-raising and cultural affairs. Some power brokers in Jewish organizations may be responding to the feminist requests. In New York City, for example, Elaine Winick and Lilliane Winn became the first two-woman team to solicit men for money.[13] Winick was Special Gifts Chairman in New York and successfully raised funds for the campaign. Allowing women to solicit businessmen was considered a major break with tradition, possibly a first step toward an integrated fund-raising structure that allows both men and women to participate equally.

At least partially because the Jewish Federation chapters are male-dominated, the exclusively Jewish women's organizations have taken on a new assertiveness and pride. Hadassah, the single largest organization with a membership of over 350,000, is actively recruiting women of all ages and assuring them that they can gain valuable experience in various areas of leadership training, organizational management, and personal satisfaction by working for Hadassah. Of course, the same ideals and goals that informed Hadassah in the 1910s still prevail. Devotion to Hadassah Hospital in Jerusalem and the various medical services and agencies provided by Hadassah in Israel remain key reasons for the Jewish American women's efforts.

Being the national president of Hadassah resembles being the president of a major corporation. The Hadassah president must supervise a multimillion-dollar yearly budget, a constituency of over 350,000 members, a national board, and thirty regional presidents. There are also twelve chapter presidents representing major cities in the country. Hadassah's president speaks for the organization at various national and local forums, confers with American Jewish leaders of other organizations, and acts as the primary spokeswoman for Hadassah in America. It is clearly a full-time responsibility. Indeed, women who become chapter presidents in cities such as Los Angeles, Chicago, and New York also work long hours.

The full-time volunteer activist fulfills all of the responsibilities and activities of a full-time administrator for a profit-making establishment, with the only vital difference being that she is not paid for her efforts. Some estimates suggest that an experienced volunteer in a major social-service agency or national Jewish organization would be paid $75,000 a year if she were in private industry. In a recent speech, sociologist Cynthia Fuchs Epstein described a women's organization she worked for; though she mentioned no names, the organization sounded very much like Hadassah:

> I spent three years with an organization which raised millions of dollars a year for hospitals and training programs. The women at the top were high-powered executive types. They came in early in the morning and left late at night; they vied for power and control of the organization; they had strong ambitions of a personal nature and also for the organization. Although they were counted by the U.S. Census as housewives, since they did not work for money, they were as involved and active as any IBM executive.[14]

The multigenerational membership within all Jewish organizations is another new development of the 1960s and 1970s. The Hannah Solomons and Henrietta Szolds created their organizations and found their major supporters among women over forty-five years old. Junior Hadasah was begun in the 1920s in recognition of potential members among unmarried young women, but most other Jewish women's organizations as well as community groups did not concern themselves with the various age groups. In recent years, there are far fewer young, unmarried Jewish women working in the factories, while there are far more young, married, middle-class women, both professional workers and homemakers. Women in their twenties, thirties, forties, and fifties are all members of Hadassah as well as contributors to the UJA.

The exclusively Jewish women's organizations have taken

cognizance of this sociological fact. Local chapters of the National Council of Jewish Women and Hadassah, for example, are organized around age groupings as well as interest groups. Young homemakers in one geographical area form a chapter of Hadassah while a group of professional women form another. There is a great deal of autonomy within each group as to programming, though the key fund-raising events of each calendar year are shared by all chapters.

Jewish women's organizations face the future with confidence. The Jewish American commitment to Israel assures support for Hadassah and Women's American ORT. The UJA Drives continue to attain their financial goals, though fund-raising continues to be a difficult battle. The immediate future, however, is not without its problems. Jewish feminists may find Hadassah a more satisfying experience for women than participation in Federation activities, but they will continue to work for expanded goals within the Jewish women's organization. B'nai B'rith Women, the National Council of Jewish Women, the National Federation of Temple Sisterhoods, Women's American ORT, and the Women's League for Conservative Judaism had supported ERA before Hadassah did so.

Will Hadassah and other Jewish women's organizations identify with other feminist issues in the 1980s? Will they support abortion rights for women? The answers are unclear for many reasons. Many religiously oriented Jewish women question whether private religious decisions should become public issues. Some Hadassah leaders believe that any attention given to feminism detracts from their primary goal: raising money for Hadassah medical projects in Israel. One of the major reasons for Hadassah's success, argue some of its supporters, has been its single-mindedness, its narrow focus upon the goals first established by Henrietta Szold. Any attention, energy, and organizational activity given to feminist projects may result in membership loss rather than gain.

In the Women's Divisions of the Jewish Federation chapters, some Jewish feminists may assert their wishes to participate more actively in decision making in the 1980s. In the areas of Jewish education and family counseling, many women may wish to play active roles in board policy making. Because Jewish women have acted as volunteers in the Jewish Sunday schools as well as in the children's and family agencies of the Federation, they have an intimate knowledge of those respective activities. Making major decisions as to use of funds and future directions may become a high-priority item for Jewish feminists interested in using their ability to serve their Jewish community. Doris Gold, a frequent writer on the subject of women volunteers, implored Jewish women volunteers to assert their expertise and stop deferring to male board chairmen.[15]

More flexible models are also becoming apparent. Jewish women volunteers participate in Jewish communal activities at some points in their adult lives, shift into professional work for a while, and then return to the volunteer sector. Others participate in both volunteer and professional activities simultaneously. Young Jewish mothers may learn about Jewish education from volunteer activities in their synagogue and use that experience to become a professional religious-school teacher or, at a later point, become a board member of the local Board of Jewish Education. All of these, and other combinations are becoming more and more common in the Jewish community. This diversity represents a healthy and respectful belief in the importance of Jewish communal work, whether it be professional or volunteer.

A third consideration that will have to be faced in the 1980s is whether continued funding from public monies and nonsectarian sources will destroy or at least dissipate the Jewish affiliation of the Jewish social-service agencies. Although the clientele of most Jewish-agency activity already includes non-Jews, there is a theoretical commitment to a Jewish focus for Jewish clients. In the case of the mammoth resettlement programs for Soviet Jews that are currently being carried out in Jewish communities all over the country, a good deal of the funding comes from governmental sources. Can it be used for Jewish education? Presently, the Jewish community assumes the cost for the latter, but with rising costs and limited funding sources, this will surely become a problem area in the near future. What role will Jewish women volunteers play, if any, in this issue? If Jewish women are to continue to be the mainstay of their families, the preservers of Jewish ritual and tradition, then they will have a particular obligation to perpetuate the Jewish ingredient in their Jewish communal activities.

Finally, will a declining economy make the Jewish commitment, and the American commitment, to philanthropy a vanishing phenomenon? Jews have always shared in the financial responsibility of caring for the members of their own community. Americans have been among the most generous givers to charities and philanthropies of any country in the world. Can these traditions continue in the face of rising inflation, uncertain futures, and troublesome foreign affairs?

6. Jewish Women Writers

Jewish women writers represent another part of the public record of Jewish women's lives. As creative artists, their work reveals both private and social struggles reshaped through unique intelligences. The fictional stories they create offer the reader a different angle of vision. While the sociological and historical accounts of Jewish women's lives offer important and authentic records, so does the imaginative prose of the Jewish women writers. Further, Jewish women writers deal with psychic and emotional realities often unexpressed in historical accounts. Imaginative writing uncovers the dialogues and the thoughts of people, the values and the tensions among them.

Jewish women writers are also worthy of inclusion in this study as examples of a successful group of professional Jewish women. They join a long list of women writers, English and American, who wrote about the private and the domestic lives of people, and about family life, interpersonal relationships, and lost loves. The group of writers included in this chapter were selected because their writings dealt with the tensions of being both Jewish and American. It is precisely their imaginative ways of working out the struggles and frustrations of livng in two cultures that make them worthy of study in this context. While the public lives of Jewish women unionists, radicals, and volunteers demonstrated their clear commitment to their Jewish heritage in an American setting, Jewish American women writers, because they are artists, have the exceptional ability to articulate both their personal concerns as well as Everyone's traumas.

There are at least three definitions of a Jewish writer: the Nazi definition, the religious definition, and the cultural definition. The Nazi definition is one in which the Jewish writer is so identified based solely upon the writer's ancestry. The content or style of the writer's work is irrelevant to this definition. The religious definition applies to Jewish writers whose stories deal with explicitly Jewish thematic material such as the concept of the Messiah, the covenantal relationship between man and God and man *and man*, and the Jewish concern with justice and righteousness. The cultural definition encompasses Jewish stories that deal with Jewish characters, pastrami sandwiches, the problems of assimilation in America, and the conflicts between the immigrant generation and their progeny.

I am employing the cultural definition for most of the Jewish women writers included in this discussion. Their stories focus upon the problems of traditional Jews in modern America and the temptations luring them away from their religion and their culture. I do not include any Jewish women writers merely because they are Jewish, the Nazi definition. Determining what is a Jewish story, however, remains a most difficult enterprise. Robert Alter has written:

> We have to remind ourselves that the so-called American Jewish writers are—with rare exceptions—culturally American in all important respects and only peripherally or vestigially Jewish.[1]

Cynthia Ozick has a more stringent definition of a Jewish story as

> one that is somehow impregnated with the values of *Judaism*, whether in the sense of that which lies between man and God or that which lies between man and man, or that which is negated in either relation. This is not to demand that Jewish content be exalted or "religious"—not at all, particularly not in any narrow pietistic meaning: but there is something far, far richer to hand than the pastrami sandwich as a means of expressing what Jewish life is, or has, among us, become.[2]

While Alter sees few Jewish American writers, Ozick's view is that neither the dialogue nor the characters have to be explicitly Jewish; in her view Saul Bellow is one of the few Jewish American writers today though his fiction does not necessarily deal with Jews specifically. In Ozick's view it is the theological framework of the story, the approach to human problems, and the solutions proposed that define a story as Jewish.

Although I find this definition intriguing, I do not accept it for the following discussion for a few reasons. First, it discounts the "cultural" Jewish stories, stories that deal with pastrami and Goldberg characters and Lower East Side settings. I think these stories are significant because they provide imaginative treatments by Jews about Jews, as they perceive them. Second, many Jewish

American women writers, born into Jewish households where the identification with Judaism was minimal at best, did not possess the scholarly learning and the theological framework desired by Ozick as an essential qualification for being Jewish. Many Jews, particularly Jewish women poorly educated in Judaism, know dimly that their Jewishness sets them apart from others but they have no significant understanding of the covenantal relationship. They are not learned in Torah and Talmud. Indeed, their fiction is sometimes an exploration into self-knowledge as well as into their social and cultural context.

A woman writer who was born to a Jewish family but does not discuss explicitly Jewish themes or introduce Jewish characters in her work does not qualify as a Jewish American writer. The point of view of Jewish woman writers, of course, varies greatly as there is no single Jewish woman's point of view. For some Jewish women writers, being a woman is more significant than being Jewish, a perspective that would make Cynthia Ozick reject the writer out of hand. But the fact that an imaginative Jewish woman writer holds that perspective does say something about her perception of herself within the Jewish and American culture, and that perception is worthy of note. To Ozick, an essential part of the writer's Jewishness is his or her awareness of the consequences of human actions. Surely this is a philosophical position inherent in Judaism but it is not unique to Judaism.

Jewish women writers occupy multiple traditions simultaneously: the American tradition of popular women writers, the male Jewish tradition of scholarship, and the literary tradition of women writers. Twentieth-century Jewish women writers participate in these three traditions and do so with ease and competence. There have been at least three generations of them in the century and their contribution to Jewish American and American literature has been significant, though often ignored in male literary histories. Indeed, Jewish women writers have been among the most successful popular writers in this country. They have displayed an uncanny ability to integrate their unique experience with the common experience of all Americans.

Women writers have thrived in this country as popularizers of American attitudes and values since the late eighteenth century. Susannah Rowson's best seller, *Charlotte Temple*, (1794) established a successful formula which has flourished ever since. Hawthorne wished his novels sold as well as those of Susan Warner and Mrs.

E.D.E.N. Southworth. The popular women novelists expressed the traditional values of America and did so in melodramatic terms: woman's purity was to be preserved before marriage, and good triumphed over evil. Women writers specialized in describing the feelings of their heroines, in emphasizing human interrelationships, and in exploring domestic trials and tribulations. The heroines—and most women writers always starred women in their stories—were all long-suffering, self-sacrificing, and stoical. They always endured, though rarely prevailed.

Scholarship has always been respected in the Jewish tradition. Although it was viewed as an exclusively male domain, Jews have looked with awe upon biblical commentators, Talmudic scholars, and learned rabbis. Judaism has been an ever-evolving religion, and major contributors to that evolution have been Torah and Talmudic scholars who have interpreted the Law in the perspective of changing times. True, medieval Jewry in Eastern Europe viewed the accumulated writings of the Talmud as the definitive word on Jewish law and custom, but the radical changes of the modern world, most notably the philosophy of the Enlightenment and the French Revolution, required a new look at traditional sources. Reform Judaism, for one, resulted from the fresh appraisal of the relationship between Judaism and the Christian world that occurred once Jews were granted civil rights in Western Europe. In the United States, Jewish intellectuals, scholars, rabbis, and writers have continued to explain Judaism to their constituency.

Further, storytelling became a most popular way of conveying Jewish values to ordinary folk. First in Yiddish and then in English, Sholom Aleichem, a nineteenth-century European Jew, told his stories to American Jews. Factual and fictional truths were conveyed through the narrative form. Isaac Bashevis Singer, a contemporary storyteller, fits into this rich tradition. Jewish writers such as Saul Bellow and Bernard Malamud have extended their storytelling to Gentile audiences as well.

The titles of some of Sholom Aleichem's stories aptly demonstrate not only the fact that males wrote most of the stories, but that they wrote primarily about men. "Yossele Solovay," "Menachem Mendl," "Tevya the Dairyman," and "Mottl Paysie, the Cantor's Son" represent Sholom Aleichem's best-known works and they all center around the lives of men. Among the works of American Yiddish writers such as Abraham Reisin and Leon Kobrin a few women appear, though they are either struggling working girls who display the difficulties faced by workers or old immigrant women, such as in Kobrin's "Bubba Basha's Turk," who have an impossible time adjusting to the New World. The assumption of both Jewish and Christian male writers that men's lives are infinitely more interesting and important than women's is clearly revealed in Yiddish writers' work as well as contemporary Jewish male writing. In the stories of Norman Mailer, Saul Bellow, and Philip Roth, for example, their heroes' plight occupies center stage. The women are usually portrayed in stereotypic fashion and play an ancillary role.

The third essential tradition shared by twentieth-century Jewish women writers is that of the uniquely female novel or short story. Since Jane Austen successfully solidified the tradition, women novelists have written stories of manners, domestic novels that described the interrelationships between men and women. The geographic sphere of the woman's novel was largely restricted to the home, and the emotional discoveries of the woman provided the central focus and drama of the story. Although female novelists were often denigrated by male literary critics, they persisted in describing the human truths they knew about; they wrote prolifically about the courtship experience, the disappointments of marriage, and the generational conflicts. Austen, George Eliot, the Brontë sisters, and Virginia Woolf were joined in this country by Edith Wharton, Ellen Glasgow, Mary Wilkins Freeman, Eudora Welty and many others. Jewish American women writers have carved out a significant part of this genre for themselves; their family stories, particularly their mother-daughter stories, deserve recognition as an important contribution to the tradition of the "domestic" novel.

Jewish women writers fit into all three traditions, with their Jewishness and femaleness supplying rich ingredients for their fictional and nonfictional creations. The American environment, of course, offers the exciting and often perplexing foundation for the writer's imagination. From this complex mixture of influences have emerged some of America's most successful women writers; few can rival Edna Ferber and Fannie Hurst as popular articulators of the American woman's life and experiences. Both Ferber and Hurst combined their Jewish background with their feminist concerns within the American context to produce effective and commercially successful fiction. America encouraged, or at least allowed, women to write and to earn a living by their writing. This opportunity was perceived by many women, Jewish and Christian alike, and enabled women to achieve economic self-sufficiency in a creative and individual way, one of the few such paths available to women.

Jewish women writers blend the various influences of which they are products. They know the experience of being different by being both women and Jews; they empathize with human suffering for both reasons as well. They share with the Jewish radicals already described a sense of marginality, of being outsiders looking in. The dilemma of being an intelligent Jewish woman in a culture that did not encourage female scholarship was not overlooked by these women. Some Jewish women writers emerged from poor, working-class families and understood the desperation of scarcity. They were keen observers of human behavior, a trait born of both heredity and cultural conditioning. As Jews, they viewed individuals as part of a social fabric, as being inextricably associated with others. This perspective had positive and negative characteristics: by being a part of a larger whole, one can gain security and confidence; by being a member of a discriminated-against, downtrodden group within the whole, one can feel ashamed, defeated, and deprived. By viewing the individual as part of his or her community, the Jewish writer also placed the individual within the community. A reciprocal relationship existed.

Self-identity, a persistent theme of twentieth-century fiction, is also discussed, described, and struggled with in Jewish women's fiction in various ways. Can an individual's identity be separated from her Jewish identity or her female identity? How can a Jewish woman fulfill her unique identity within the traditional Jewish culture? Muriel Rukeyser, in a poem entitled "To Be a Jew in the Twentieth Century," has put it thus:

To be a Jew in the twentieth century
Is to be offered a gift. If you refuse,
Wishing to be invisible, you choose
Death of the spirit, the stone insanity.[3]

Rukeyser's view is not necessarily shared by all Jewish women writers. Some of the women writers described dealt with Jewishness as seen through the eyes of Jewish men, not women. All, however, include Judaism as an integral part of their fictional world in at least some of their work.

The following discussion of Jewish women writers is based on a selection of writers and their stories. The reader can surely find other examples of Jewish women writers who fit into the thematic categories described or who diverge significantly from them. Jewish American women writers write about both their private sorrows and public concerns; their work often expresses repetitive and universal subjects. The first generation's problems with assimilation, for example, written about from the perspective of the 1970s, take on a different cast from a treatment in a similar story written in the 1910s. The fact that the theme of adjustment is explored over and over in each generation suggests that it is unfinished business, an issue which subsequent generations have not effectively resolved.

The interest in origins typical of the 1960s and 1970s also manifests itself in Jewish Americn fiction. The retracing of steps and the returning to the immigrant generation to determine the source of self as well as the roots of anxiety are frequent themes. Other major fictional themes are: how self-willed Jewish women separate themselves from their autocratic fathers; how the two generations coexist; how immigrants adjust to the bewildering life in America; how Jews try to remain religious in secular America; and how the heroines resolved, or at least, came to terms with the challenge of being Jewish American women. Jewish women born in America at the end of the last century as well as those born in the 1920s and 1930s have asked and answered many of the same questions. The significant fact that Jews are raised in a culture that treasures the family structure plays an important role in all of the literary treatments. Even when the Jewish woman writer satirizes the Jewish family, she still remains a part of what is satirized. Gail Parent, a good example of this approach, can never rid herself of the Jewish parents whom she sees as burdensome. The omnipresent Jewish family remains a persistent shadow.

Indeed, family stories dominate the output of Jewish women writers. From Thyra Samter Winslow's "A Cycle of Manhattan" (1923) to Gail Parent's *David Meyer Is a Mother* (1977), Jewish women writers have been concerned with creating in artful form a description, an explanation, a dramatic rendering, and an exorcism of children's relationships to parents and of the meaning of the Jewish family in the lives of the children. While Jewish American male writers have also been concerned with this theme, the Jewish women writers offer at least two original perspectives on the subject: they usually focus upon the lives of daughters rather than sons, and they display more sympathy and empathy for all of the parties involved.

Native Jewish American writers like Thyra Samter Winslow (1895–1961) and Fannie Hurst (1889–1968) were observers of the immigrant family, not participants. Both came from German Jewish families, Hurst grew up in St. Louis and Winslow in Fort Smith, Arkansas. They wrote about the New York City immigrant experience as outsiders observing a foreign and dying culture. Their sentimental sympathies, however, were with the older generation. As they were not a part of the culture, no emotional grappling between the generations is portrayed in their fiction. Rather, they present humane portraits of a way of life that is declining. The writers both believe in the worth of that decaying culture, but both can only hint at its positive features.

In "A Cycle of Manhattan," Winslow described an immigrant family named Rosenheimer. Mr. Rosenheimer, a struggling tailor, succeeds as a garment manufacturer. In the process, he changes his name to Ross, moves from MacDougal Street in Greenwich Village to a home on Long Island as well as one on East Sixty-fifth Street. His five children quickly adapt to the rich, good life. Irving changes his name to Irwin, Mannie to Manning, and Carolyn to Carrie. The portrait is not an attractive one. The women in the family become grasping, vain, and snobbish; the men become greedy and ambitious. The only person who retains her integrity and identity is the Grandma, Mrs. Ross' mother, who refuses to remove her *sheitel* ("wig") and continues to speak in Yiddish. In the ironic conclusion, the family visits the youngest son in his new Greenwich Village loft, only to discover that it is the site of the parents' first apartment in New York.

In another story, "Grandma," a good-humored seventy-three-year-old grandmother who divides the year into visits with each of her three children and their families discovers that the most pleasant part of each visit is the train ride between places. The rich son's house is cold and formal; another child is stubborn and inhospitable; and the third son, Fred, whose home is the warmest, is a failure in business and expects Grandma to work long hours during her visits. In both of these stories, Winslow introduces the perspective of the older person with dignity. Contrary to the dominant trend of youthful heroes and heroines, Winslow's grandparents present an often overlooked point of view. She had no solutions to the dilemma, no easy answers for achieving intergenerational harmony, but she provided an early statement on the gap that was developing between the immigrant and subsequent generations as well as between the old and the young perspectives.

Fannie Hurst's story "The Gold in Fish" (1927) offers a witty and compassionate treatment of the struggles between the generations. Mr. and Mrs. Goldfish have three children; their son Morris has become a successful auctioneer and the opening scene of the story has Morris announcing that he has changed the family name to Fish. Mrs. Goldfish is confused and doubtful: "You hear that, papa. The name that was good enough for you to get born into, and for me to marry into, is something to be ashamed of."[4] Birdie, the unmarried, overweight daughter of the family (Hurst's voice), supplies the humor and the sarcasm:

> Goldfish is a liability, is it? Well, how's gefuldte fish? Morris Gefuldte Fish. At least when you were amputating why didn't you cut off the tail, you poor Fish, and leave the Gold?[5]

Morris wins his parents over, but his search for respectability is endangered when Birdie marries a shady character who is sent to prison for selling "hot" merchandise.

Mr. Goldfish becomes seriously ill, calls for Birdie, and tells her:

> I'm an old man, Birdie. They let me get into an old man before my time, from not having enough in my life to make it worth while I should want to live on. I got good children, Birdie, but I been lonesome for my business—Birdie—for you—...[6]

Mr. Goldfish dies and Birdie takes her mother with her to her modest apartment in the Bronx, away from the modish Upper West Side. In the Bronx, Mrs. Goldfish can cook her garlicky foods and her Old World specialties. Birdie emerges as the respector of tradition as well as the realist. She says of herself at one point: "I'm low-brow maybe, but thank God, not browbeaten."[7] On another occasion, she tells her brother Morris:

> Why, ma and pa used to be two individuals before you set about killing them with kindness. Before you took the Goldfish family out of water. . . .I know every time ma puts a hat on her head it gives her a headache. I know how she goes on the sly and buys herself a miltz and sneaks in the kitchen on the cook's day out to fix it for her and pa. I know how pa'd rather haggle selling a secondhand, golden-pak, roller-top, Grand Rapids desk to Jacob Mintz than sit sunning himself all day in a Heppelwhite chair, that he cannot pronounce.[8]

"The Gold in Fish" is representative of the Jewish-immigrant-assimilation story. Its dialogue is sharp and pointed; its characters realistic. The sympathies lie with the old people, the Old-World representatives somewhat bewildered by their successful children in the New World. The confrontation between the two cultures is not an even match. The older generation is not equipped to defend its way of life against secular, materialistic America. And so they lose the battle.

It is interesting to note, however, that neither Winslow nor Hurst depicts rebellious heroines, young women rejecting their parents' past. The rebels are male; the defenders of the tradition in "The Gold in Fish" are the women of both generations, Mrs. Goldfish and Birdie. Both of these Jewish women writers sensed the separation between the generations, the growing chasm in values and behaviors, but they chose to represent the rebellion in male terms, not female. This was both an artistically and sociologically authentic decision: readers in both the Jewish and American cultures identify more easily with male rebels; indeed, they expect men to be initiators and innovators. The majority of breaks with Jewish tradition were among the men. Jewish men, until recently, married outside the faith in far greater numbers than Jewish women. Jewish men gave up religious practices because they had to work on the Sabbath. Thus, more Jewish male characters in fiction defied their parents than did female characters.

At least one immigrant woman writer early in the century wrote of heroines who desperately tried to free themselves from tyrannical fathers. Anzia Yezierska's (1880–1970) stories usually contained a scholarly but autocratic father, a mother worn down by a large family and economic deprivation, and many children struggling to be free of their father. In *Bread Givers*, Sara Smolinsky is determined not to follow her sisters in marrying the man of their father's choice. She breaks away from her family, lives on her own, works, studies, and finally becomes a teacher. She meets her father at the end of the story when she is about to marry the school principal. Sara's mother has died and her father has married a demanding woman; he is now reduced to peddling on the street:

What's an old father to heartless American children? Have they any religion? Any fear of God? Do they know what it means, "Honour thy father"? What else can I do to support myself and her? She drove me out to bring her in money.[9]

In a rare happy ending, Sara reconciles with her father and her fiancé expresses an interest in studying Hebrew with him. The Old World and the New World join together harmoniously. Usually Yezierska's heroines strive for a free and independent life but do not achieve it. In "Hunger," a story in her collection *Hungry Hearts* (1920), Shenah Pessah leaves her autocratic uncle and gets a job in a factory. Although a kind coworker named Sam Arkin falls in love with her and wants to marry her, she rejects him because she wants to succeed on her own.

> But only—there is something—... it lifts me on top of my hungry body—the hunger to make from myself a person that can't be crushed by nothing nor nobody—the life higher!

She then tells Sam: "Give yourself your own strength."[10]

In contrast to Winslow's and Hurst's heroines, Yezierska's women display a feminist sense of independence and an "unfeminine" wish to rebel. Indeed, Yezierska is enjoying a renaissance of interest in the 1970s and 1980s precisely because her women reject male authority and seek personal forms of expression. While the feminist interpretation is currently popular, Yezierska's heroines lived in the Jewish immigrant context; their rebellion was expressed against a religion, a male tradition, and a way of life that prescribed adult-life patterns for all women, with no deviation allowed. It is the rigidity of the traditional Jewish script that inspired Yezierska's greatest wrath. As an immigrant who shared that upbringing, her fiction rings with authenticity. While native Jewish writers such as Hurst and Winslow could empathize with the older generation trying to preserve their culture against rebellious sons, Yezierska knew the personal suffering of a bright and ambitious female wanting to shape her own life.

Jewish women writers of the middle generation, those born between 1910 and 1930, display in their fiction an emotional distance from the generational conflict. It is not always their parents who were the immigrants, but often their grandparents. Although autobiography and fiction are surely not interchangeable, the essential structure, mood, and values of the imaginative writing are drawn from the personal experience of the writer. Hortense Calisher (1911–), though not well-known as a Jewish American writer, has suggested that her Elkin-family stories have a kinship to her personal life. Grace Paley (1922–), another member of this middle generation, has created a series of stories about a Jewish family named Darwin in which the older generation, now retired and living in a Jewish retirement home, remains vital and feisty. Tillie Olsen's (1913–) best-known work, *Tell Me a Riddle*, also fits into this category. Knowingly or unknowingly, all three writers express sympathy born from separation. They describe the culture of the grandparents' generation with humane respect but also with a realistic awareness of the passing of their value system.

The middle generation, however, shares with the first generation, and the subsequent one, concern with families and connections. The protagonist in each and every story is interested in knowing her origins so that she can work out her own synthesis. In the cases where the heroines are not necessarily in personal conflict, the search for the past acts as an explicator, a means of solving some puzzle. For Paley, the explorations are not satisfying. Daughter Faith Darwin learns little that aids her in dealing with her problematic life. Her parents' answers offer little comfort or explanation to her. Similarly, in Olsen's *Tell Me a Riddle*, it is the third generation, represented by the granddaughter, that benefits from the encounter with the older generation. The multigenerational view seems appropriate for writers concerned with the family who have living parents and children. They are located in the middle, as is their fiction.

Hortense Calisher has written a series of short stories about a German Jewish family called the Elkins. The Elkins operate under a series of burdens: the presence of the family matriarch, Mrs. Elkins, who controls the purse strings; a Jewish heritage that everyone is trying to forget; and business reverses that cause tensions between Mr. and Mrs. Elkins. The stories are often told from the point of view of Hester, the daughter. In "The Gulf Between," Hester overhears a quarrel between her parents:

> On the one side stood her mother, the denying one, the unraveler of other people's facades, but resolute and forceful by her very lack of some dimension; on the other side stood her father, made weak by his awareness of others, carrying like phylactery the burden of his kindness. And flawed with their difference, she felt herself falling endlessly, soundlessly, in the gulf between.[11]

Calisher characterizes Mr. Elkin's burden as "phylactery," the male Jew's prayer clothing, and Hester's personality is split down the middle. The connection with Judaism is viewed as a connection with weakness.

In "Old Stock," Mrs. Elkin and fifteen-year-old Hester go to a summer resort in the Catskills. They stay at an old farm, away from the flashy resorts frequented by most Jews. "For Mrs. Elkin walked through the world swinging the twangy words 'refined,' 'refinement,' like a purifying censer before her."[12] When a woman makes an anti-Semitic remark to Mrs. Elkin about another guest, Hester watches carefully to see how her mother will handle the situation. Mrs. Elkin says quietly that she is a Hebrew. Hester thinks:

> Please say it, Mother. Say "Jew". She heard the word in her own mind, double-voiced, like the ram's horn at Yom Kippur, with an ugly present bray but with a long, urgent echo as time-spanning as Roland's horn.[13]

At fifteen, Hester senses her mother's shame and hesitancy to acknowledge her Jewishness. Mrs. Elkin does not deny it, but neither does she assert it proudly. Judaism never plays a major role in Hester's life, although she seems to intuit that one cannot hide a part of oneself.

In "The Middle Drawer," Hester appears as a married woman with a child of her own who returns to her parents' home after her mother's death of cancer at the age of fifty-eight. She contemplates opening the middle drawer of her mother's dresser, a drawer that held many childhood memories for her. She reviews her mother's life as well as the icy truce she shared with her. She ruefully concludes that she will spend the rest of her life trying to obtain her dead mother's approval. Calisher's Elkin-family stories explore the sources of individual identity and the role that Judaism plays in it. There is never a satisfactory resolution. Intergenerational conflict persists, as do mother-daughter conflicts.

Grace Paley, a contemporary Jewish woman writer, is also preoccupied with the family theme. Out of twenty-seven stories published in her two collections of stories (*The Little Disturbances of Man* and *Enormous Changes At The Last Minute*), ten deal with a Jewish family named Darwin. Paley's vision is wry and ironic. She looks carefully and cleverly at the seamy, the sentimental, and the heroic sides of working-class Jewish life. In contrast to most Jewish women writers, she concentrates on the lives of poor Jews. Her characters struggle to survive in a disappointing world. Crazy and unusual experiences confront them; lovers disappoint them; and they do not achieve the American promise of happiness.

Paley's Darwin stories often focus upon the daughter, Faith, whose name belies her grasp on reality. She has no faith in herself or her ability to cope effectively. Her worthless husband Ricardo has abandoned her and her sons Anthony and Richard. She continually seeks guidelines from her parents, the passersby in the park, and her old neighbors. No one seems to provide her with the needed structure or advice. "You should get help," her sister Hope tells her in "Faith in the Afternoon."

> "Psychiatry was invented for people like you, Faithful," says Charles. [her brother] "My little blondie, life is short. I'll lay out a certain amount of cash," says her father. "When will you be a person," says her mother.[14]

While her parents worry about the partitioning of Jerusalem, Faith worries about herself. In "Faith in a Tree," she wonders why her mother sent her on an airplane ride alone when she was a child:

> What was my mother trying to prove? That I was independent? That she wasn't the sort to hang on? That in the sensible, socialist, Zionist world of the future she wouldn't cry at my wedding? "You're an American child. Free. Independent."[15]

In "The Long-Distance Runner," Faith becomes a jogger and runs to her old neighborhood, hoping to find answers:

> A woman inside the streamy energy of middle age runs and runs. She finds the houses and streets where her childhood happened. She lives in them. She learns as though she was still a child what in the world is coming next.[16]

Faith remains without answers but she continues the habit of philosophizing. Her son Richard, in "Faith in a Tree," tells her to "quit with your all-the-time philosophies," [17] but she ignores his advice and continues to puzzle over her problems. "If it's truth and honor you want to refine," Faith muses, "I think the Jews have some insight. Make no images, imitate no God. After all, in His field, the graphic arts, He is preeminent."[18]

In "Faith in the Afternoon," neither Faith nor Hope can under-

stand why their parents chose to live in the Children of Judea retirement home:

> "Now, Mother, how will you make out with all those *yentas*? Some
> of them don't even speak English." "I have spoken altogether too
> much English in my life," said Mrs. Darwin. "If I really liked
> English that much, I would move to England." "Why don't you go
> to Israel?" asked Charles. "That would at least make sense to
> people." "And leave you?" she asked, tears in her eyes at the
> thought of them alone, wrecking their lives on the shoals of every
> day, without her tearful gaze attending.[19]

Paley's brilliant dialogue and characterization evoke images of tor-
tured people (especially Faith) struggling with the day-to-day problems that most people take for granted. The Darwins' commitment
to Zionism and their belief in socialism and Yiddish culture seem to
have little, if any, influence upon Faith, Hope, and Charles. Faith's
sons listen impatiently to her stories of the past and see little connection with their lives. Anthony spends each weekend visiting his
friends in various state institutions.

Faith Darwin is a liberal who empathizes with the plight of all of
the downtrodden. She marches for the right causes, tolerates the ir-
responsibility of the men in her life, is permissive with her children,
and reviews her past with compulsive regularity. Her parents' commitments have become secularized in her scheme of living; their
Zionist-socialist philosophy has become a leftist critique of
materialism. She no longer identifies with Israel but with all of
humanity. Her Judaism has become humanism.

Tillie Olsen's *Tell Me a Riddle*, like Winslow's "Grandma," gives
the reader the older generation's perspective. Eva and David, an old
married couple, have lived and suffered together for forty-seven
years. David wants to sell their home and move to the Haven, a
cooperative for the aged provided by his Lodge. Eva wants to remain
in their home. He tries to persuade her:

> A reading circle. Chekhov they read that you like, and Peretz.
> Cultured people at the Haven that you would enjoy.
>
> "Enjoy!" She tasted the word. "Now, when it pleases you, you
> find a reading circle for me. And forty years ago when the
> children were morsels and there was a Circle, did you stay home

with them once so I could go? Even once? You trained me well. I do not need others to enjoy."[20]

The old couple are cultural Jews, not religious ones. When Eva gets sick toward the end of the story and the rabbi visits her in the hospital, she rails against his presence and instructs her children: "Tell them to write: Race, human; Religion, none."[21]

In her frequent monologues, Eva appears as a sensitive intellectual whose channels of communication were stifled by the demands of child rearing and a culture that favored men's intellectual development. Ironically, in defiance of all expectations, her children have continued the Jewish rituals which she had abandoned. Her children wanted her to be like the other grandparents who observed tradition. Like Faith Darwin, Eva is a humanist; she believes in obliterating religious differences and creating common human bonds.

> Heritage. How have we come from our savage past, how no longer to be savages—this to teach. To look back and learn what humanizes—this to teach.[22]

Tell Me a Riddle is a masterful portrait of three generations of American Jews seen through the eyes of Eva, David, their children, and their granddaughter Jeannie. Jeannie nurses her grandmother during her final illness and offers Eva a youthful and vital companion in her final days. Eva is the center of the story, and it is her vision of her life—how it was spent in traditional maternal and wifely pursuits—that consumes the narrative. Judaism does not provide her with solace or an explanation for her life. The constant dialetic among Eva's thoughts, her husband's, her children's, and others, gives the story a power, tension, and dynamism that is rare in fiction. Eva is both the product of her culture as well as its chief critic. She never accepts her fate and pursues an active mental debate with all around her. The barriers between Eva and David, between her sensibility and her culture, have never been broken down. She dies without changing anyone's mind or anyone's perceptions of her. David "wept as if there never would be tears enough," but Jeannie comforts him: "Granddaddy, it is all right. She promised me. Come back, come back and help her poor body to die."[23]

Tell Me a Riddle occupies a unique position in contemporary American fiction in that old people are rarely the central characters of American fiction, and an old heroic Jewish woman is a rarity. Olsen's Eva is vibrant, combative, and thoughtful. She questions her heritage and her children's lives. She appears as an inimitable character who never lived the life she wished but never despaired or wallowed in self-pity. In the end, the reader does not pity her, but rather admires her adamant adherence to her own views. Eva survived as a singular thinker who kept her own counsel, but kept it well.

The third generation of Jewish women writers, those born in the 1930s and 1940s, have lost both sympathy and understanding for the immigrant generation, traditional Jewish religion, and the secular Yiddish culture. It is no longer exotic, intriguing, or enlightening to search for one's Jewish past; it is only troublesome. Rona Jaffe (1932–) and Gail Parent (1940–), two good examples of this generation of writers, portray the Jewish American families as materialistic, devoid of values, and desperately in search of the next status symbol. From their point of view, the heritage that the parents and grandparents gave the third generation consisted only of neuroses to unravel and identity crises to overcome.

Popular, contemporary writer Rona Jaffe's *Family Secrets* (1974) is a good example of the third generation's contribution to the Jewish-family genre. *Family Secrets* is the story of patriarch Adam Saffron, self-made immigrant millionaire, who fathers six children by two marriages and lives to see the grandchildren rebel against their parents and him. Although Bar Mitzvahs and Jewish holidays are celebrated, the connection with the religious Jewish culture is tenuous at best. Grandson Richie, for example, studies to be a rabbi, but three months before his ordination, quits because he is no longer eligible for the draft. Adam's material success and assimilation into upper-class American life is the ostensible reason given by Jaffe for the family's falling away from Judaism.

Among Adam's six children, one son marries a Gentile, one demented daughter marries a "no-goodnik," and one son becomes "Frenchified" when he marries a French wife. The grandchildren offer little hope for the future. Of the nine grandchildren, one becomes a flower child, one becomes a runner, and the others become all-American achievers. Jaffe's portrait of three generations of a Jewish American family is bleak. The connections to Judaism have all but faded with the third generation. Indeed, there is not even a curiosity, let alone any anxiety, about the connections between the Jewish past and the present.

Gail Parent's two humorous novels, *Sheila Levine Is Dead and Living in New York* (1972) and *David Meyer is a Mother* (1977), both fit into this thematic type. As in Jaffe's work, the families portrayed feel no positive connection with Judaism. Sheila Levine is a fat, unmarried thirty-year-old whose younger sister has already married. What is Sheila's future? Dark humor and pathos intermingle in the novel; both Sheila and her family become the objects of Parent's satire.

Sheila imagines her parents' conversation when she was born:

> "My, what a beautiful baby."...."So, it's a girl, Manny? You know what that means, you have to pay for the wedding...."One day old! One day old, and they're talking about weddings.[24]

One-liners like the ones in this dialogue are strewn throughout the story. Jewish parents are the butt of the humor; Sheila is the unwilling captive of a marriage-obsessive culture, of overly possessive parents, and of a materialistic environment. There is no positive Jewish identification, only caricatured Jewish characters. Another instance of the treatment rendered Judaism is the scene in which Sheila attends the funeral of her Aunt Goldie. Parent gives us the rabbi's eulogy:

> I never met Goldie Butkin, but I know she was a wonderful woman, for this woman was a MOTHER. A MOTHER.... A MOTHER is...a MOTHER is...like the COVER of a BOOK. The family is the book, BUT the MOTHER is the cover. I ask you, if the COVER of the BOOK, which is the MOTHER, gets worn and old, does that mean that the BOOK, which is the family, is no good? NO! The BOOK, which is the FAMILY, is still GOOD because the MOTHER has protected it...What you do is take the cover off and throw it away...but do you take the mother off...no...Maybe the mother is not like the cover of a book...Turn your prayer book to page five.[25]

Gail Parent, a professional comedy writer, obviously sees the Jewish family as an infinite source of amusement. In *David Meyer is a Mother*, she pokes fun at the "Jewish prince," the spoiled Jewish son raised in a household where his every wish is anticipated and fulfilled. David, unable to cope with women's liberation, resorts to a massage parlor-whorehouse for sexual gratification. He falls in love with a prostitute who turns out to be a nice, Jewish girl named

Linda Minsk, an undercover reporter working there for a story. In classic sex-role-reversal terms, David wants to marry Linda, who wants to remain independent; David wants to have a child while Linda does not, and David worries and worries when she does not call him.

David, though he lives in Los Angeles where he works as a television programmer, always wonders what his father, Myron Meyer, who lives in New York, thinks of him. Parent's portrait of David's parents, who come to visit him, is dipped in acid. The Meyers complain all of the time, are suspicious of everyone, and are exceedingly shallow. David's mother is a storehouse of catastrophe and disease stories and his father carries his own luggage for fear of it being stolen. Yet when David's mother dies, he becomes distraught and sentimental. He cannot live with his parents nor can he live without them. When David's father decides to move to California and quickly marries a young Gentile woman, David is horrified.

David is also ridiculed in the novel. Both generations emerge as morally, spiritually, and intellectually bankrupt. The conclusion one draws from Gail Parent's two contributions to the Jewish-family genre is that the merger between Judaism and Americanism has produced a dead end. There is nowhere to go, no vitality, and no hope for future generations of Jewish Americans in Parent's vision. A final example of the genre also demonstrates this very negative view of the Jewish family: Norma Rosen's (1925–) novella, *Green*, and her short story, "Apples." In both stories, the major characters are Jewish but their connections to Judaism are ambivalent, if not hostile. Muriel Ruznack, the protagonist in *Green*, lives in principled poverty with her artist-husband Herb and their two children. She resents her widowed sister Esther, who is planning on marrying a rich man, and she tries to prevent her husband from succumbing to commercialism. She appears as self-righteous and inflexible.

In "Apples," Larry Goldstein must be persuaded by his wife Penny to invite his widowed father for dinner and, eventually, to live with them. Larry has tried very hard to separate himself from his parents' world, from Jewish tradition, and from a Jewish identity. When his wife prepares some of her father-in-law's old favorite dishes, Larry looks at the dishes as remnants of some primitive culture: "Deep in the pot, the long thick slices of breast meat, each with three flat narrow bones protruding from their slipper envelopes of gristle."[26] The last link to his Jewishness, Jewish food, also repulses him. His father represents a way of life that he has tried to avoid. While his dead mother had always told him that the apple does not fall far from the tree, Larry muses that he has spent his energies rolling far away from the tree.

Although these members of the third generation are by no means the only ones writing on the Jewish American experience, their views on the consequences of assimilation are more representative than not. Many of the current best sellers chronicling the Jewish American story describe, in grisly detail, how the unity of the immigrant culture has been destroyed. Many Jewish American women writers have shed their Jewish identity, and concentrate instead on the woman's dilemma. They have generalized from the traditional Jewish culture to the secular American one and found both wanting.

Although much fiction is based upon autobiography, some Jewish American women writers discussed growing up Jewish in explicitly autobiographical writings. Edna Ferber (1887-1968), probably the most prominent Jewish woman writer of the first fifty years of the twentieth century, wrote two volumes of autobiography (*A Peculiar Treasure* and *A Kind of Magic*) in which she discussed her Jewish heritage and the process of growing up in small Midwestern towns. Ferber's mother, Julia, came from a middle-class, Chicago Jewish family named Neumann. She married a Hungarian Jewish immigrant, Jacob Ferber, who continually struggled to support his family. Jacob was not a good businessman, and his failing health required Julia to take over the management of the family dry-goods store. The Ferbers lived in a variety of places: Kalamazoo, Michigan (where Edna was born), Chicago (where they stayed with Edna's maternal grandparents, the Neumanns), Ottumwa, Iowa (where anti-Semitism made life miserable), and finally Appleton, Wisconsin (where Edna went to high school and her mother successfully operated a dry-goods store).

Julia Ferber became Edna's heroine. The hardy Jew and female had merged into the same figure in Ferber's life and imagination. In Ferber's 1917 novel *Fanny Herself*, which reads like a fictionalized autobiography, the setting is Winnebago, Wisconsin and the heroine is Molly Brandeis, the owner of Brandeis' Bazaar. Fanny is her thirteen-year-old daughter. The husband Ferdinand is described as "a dreamer, and a potential poet."[27] He dies early in the story and Molly proceeds to operate the business and raise Fanny and her brother Theodore. They are the only Jewish family in the community in which there is a working widow, a fact that does not go unnoticed by Winnebago's Jews. "Jewish women, they would tell you, didn't work thus. Their husbands work for them, or their sons, or their brothers."[28] Mrs. Brandeis replies to her critics:

"I seem to remember a Jewess named Ruth who was left widowed, and who gleaned in the fields for her living, and yet the neighbors didn't talk. For that matter, she seems to be pretty well thought of, to this day."[29]

Mrs. Brandeis is too busy to be concerned with catty gossip. She takes Fanny with her to Chicago on buying trips and works to care for her family. Fanny feels different from her schoolmates for two reasons: she has a working mother, and she is Jewish. Only one girl in her class stays home on the Jewish holidays. But the feeling of differentness does not turn into resentfulness. Ferber describes Fanny's impression of the Yom Kippur service in the synagogue and the recitation of the Kaddish, the prayer commemorating the dead. "There is nothing in the written language that, for sheer drama and magnificence, can equal it as it is chanted in Hebrew."[30] Fanny eventually leaves her small town and moves first to Chicago and then New York, but she never forgets her Jewish origins nor does she consciously abandon her identity.

In *A Kind of Magic*, the second volume of her autobiography, Ferber draws a connection between women and Jews, a connection that she knew from her own life experience as well as one she had witnessed. Writing about the fact that she admired women enormously and usually wrote about them, she continues:

In many important ways women are often—in fact, usually—smarter than men. The word smarter is deliberately used. They have had to be smarter in order to survive. There is little or nothing cerebral in this particular gift or trait. It is almost a reflex. They are smarter for the same reasons that Jews are often considered smarter than non-Jews. They were held in subjection because she was a female; the Jew because of his religious belief in one God only, rejecting the Jew Jesus as a divinity. Hounded and bedeviled and persecuted, granted few rights and fewer privileges, they learned—the rejected Female and rejected Jew—perforce to see through the back of their heads as well as through the front of their heads.[31]

As vulnerable people, Jews and women needed sensitivity and intelligence. Ferber's strong Jewish mother became the positive model for all of her heroines.

The truth was (and still is at this writing) that Julia Ferber as a

human being was so dimensional, sustaining, courageous and
vital that my years of close companionship with her never were
dull. . . .[32]

Gay, enormously entertaining; shrewd, intelligent, possessive, in-
tuitive, courageous, here was a protean character who, often to
my surprise and sometime annoyance, flung open the door and
marched lifesize into my novels as I wrote them.[33]

It is Julia Ferber's particular strength that becomes the prototype
for all of Ferber's heroines; it is not Julia Ferber as a Jewish woman-
mother that informs the fiction. Rather, all of the heroines find the
business of living as women, sometimes as widows with young
children (Selina DeJong in *So Big*), to be totally preoccupying. Ferber
does not place upon them the additional "burden" of Judaism. In her
own life, she retained a respect for the rich heritage of her
forebears and did not seem to find it difficult to be a writer and a
Jew. Once she exorcised her personal history in the writing of *Fanny
Herself*, Ferber rarely focuses upon a fictional description of Jews.
Occasionally a Jewish character would appear in one of her stories,
but after Fanny, Jews no longer occupied center stage in her fiction.
The woman had replaced the Jew as her central figure. Ferber's fictional universe had moved from her particular environment to a
more universal one. All women, not only the Julia Ferbers of the
world, could identify with working women, with widows, and with
women who survived multiple tragedies.
   Fannie Hurst also wrote an autobiography in which her
Jewishness played a significant role. Born in Hamilton, Ohio in 1889,
Fannie Hurst was raised in St. Louis. Her father was a successful
leather manufacturer of German Jewish descent, while her mother,
Rose Koppel, had come from a farming family and was a retiring,
traditional wife. Fannie's paternal aunts and uncles were very
status-conscious and looked disdainfully upon the newly arrived
Russian Jewish immigrants. Aunt Jennie advised the young Fannie:

Get married young. Don't educate yourself into a bluestocking.
The more you know, the less desirable you become to men. They
want a homemaker, not a superior mind.[34]

And later, when her stories were being purchased by the *Saturday
Evening Post*, her mother reminded her:

"All right, *The Saturday Evening Post* is a big thing. But do you mean to say you hesitate between such a life and a home of your own, with say a little writing on the side? That is," concluded Mamma witheringly, "unless *The Saturday Evening Post* doesn't believe in marriage."[35]

Fannie Hurst moved to New York during the 1910s and worked as a waitress and salesclerk while trying to get her stories published. She frequently walked the streets of the Lower East Side where the newly arriving immigrants lived; she also visited New York's port of entry, Ellis Island. Her writings featured women, usually working-class women whose lives were filled with abandoned lovers, illegitimate children, and large doses of suffering. Her descriptions of people and her dialogue were sharp and realistic. She apparently worked out a personal truce with her Jewish heritage and was able to write imaginative stories about women very different from the Jewish women she knew. While she spoke for Jewish causes, supported the State of Israel, and gave generously to Jewish organizations, her professional writing career was centered on the enormously successful formula fiction of melodrama.

Anzia Yezierska also wrote an autobiography called *Red Ribbon on a White Horse*, in which her real-life struggles with her father are depicted. In contrast to Hurst and Ferber, Yezierska's autobiography and her fiction merge; they both describe the same thematic conflicts, the same problems in achieving selfhood in America. Being female, ambitious, and the daughter of a traditional Jewish father were all obstacles Yezierska had to overcome. When she achieved recognition with her story "Hungry Hearts," she found fame and fortune bewildering and difficult to comprehend. Film producer Samuel Goldwyn bought the rights to the story and invited Yezierska to Hollywood to write the film script. She became confused.

Once you knew what poor people suffered it kept gnawing at you. You'd been there yourself. You wanted to reach out and help. But if you did, you were afraid you might be dragged back into the abyss.[36]

Within a year, she was back in New York writing her stories of immigrant life on the Lower East Side. Never again would she achieve the fame of Hollywood. Anzia Yezierska's short stories and novels consistently portrayed the grim conditions facing poor, unskilled Jewish immigrants. The women were doubly victimized: they were at the mercy of authoritarian fathers and husbands, and they were poorly educated because of religious ideas about their fate.

Cynthia Ozick (1928–), more than any of the other Jewish women writers discussed in this chapter, deserves special attention because she has devoted *all* of her fictional and nonfictional writing to the subject of being a Jew in America. Therefore, while our other writers often developed a Jewish theme, such as the generational conflict, Ozick explores many facets of Judaism. The question of how to practice Judaism in America, given the multiple temptations and the various interpretations, consumes her literary consciousness. In *The Pagan Rabbi and Other Stories* (1971), many of the Jewish characters struggle with their Jewish identity as well as the conflict between the past and the present. "The Pagan Rabbi," for example, is about a learned Mishnah expert whose intense studies lead him off into mystical directions. By the story's end, he loses his grasp upon reality entirely. From a theological standpoint, his downfall results from his belief in the union of the soul with nature, a pagan concept totally unacceptable to Jewish thinking.

In "Envy; or, Yiddish in America," a Yiddish poet named Edelshtein envies a fellow poet, Ostrover, who has succeeded in America. Edelshtein rages against the injustice of this man's fame while he remains in obscurity. Yiddish is dying in America and Edelshtein's work seems doomed to obscurity. His efforts to get a young woman to translate his writings into English prove futile, and Edelshtein's failure seems ensured.

In "The Doctor's Wife," a fifty-year-old, bachelor doctor skillfully avoids his three sisters' efforts to get him married.

> The doctor, it seemed, was not very attentive to his sisters. This was because they were women, and women have no categories. He did not notice his sisters as individuals, but he noticed what they were. They were free. They were free because they were unfree; they were exempt from choices. They did not have to *be* anything; it was enough that they were women. Their bodies were their life's blueprints; they married, became pregnant, nursed their infants, fussed over their children's homework.[37]

It is interesting to note that the protagonists in most of Ozick's stories are men; Jewish men have to come to terms with their

Jewishness, their adulthood, their roles in society. Women, Jewish women, at least as seen in "The Doctor's Wife," are free precisely because of their lack of freedom.

In a more recent story called "Bloodshed," Bleilip, a lawyer turned fund raiser, visits his distant cousin Toby and her husband Yussel who live in a newly created Hasidic town. Bleilip is a skeptic who has lost faith in God but remains fascinated by the fervor of the Hasidim. Toby, who had been a university student with great ambitions before marriage (she had hoped to be the first Jewish woman president), seems content to raise her four sons in this religious community. Bleilip attends the afternoon prayer service with Yussel and listens with growing discomfort to the rabbi's discussion of how the Temple priest sacrificed a goat instead of a person. Slaughter for a higher good is condoned while the rabbi discovers that Bleilip carries a gun for self protection. Bleilip confesses that, though a disbeliever, he sometimes believes, and the rabbi concludes the story by saying: "Then you are as bloody as anyone. . . "[38]

In "Usurpation," a story that shared first-place honors in the 1975 O.Henry Awards, Ozick weaves a story within a story with multiple narrators. The layers of the story become increasingly complex as the author warns the reader not to be seduced by magic. Judaism, Ozick reminds everyone, forbids the use of, or belief in, magic. Levity, she also notes, is not Torah and is therefore bad. To Ozick, God and Torah equal reality while myths and magic describe illusions. But the burden of Torah is immense.

> Someday I will take courage and throw over being a Jew, and then I will make a little god, a silver godlet, in the shape of a crown, which will stop death, resurrect fathers and uncles; within its royal points gardens will burst.[39]

The theme of throwing off the shackles of Judaism is also prominent in Ozick's nonfiction. Jews cannot be anything but Jews; yet that historical identity, that obligation, is a mighty one. In a piece written for a symposium called "Living in Two Cultures," Ozick says that "we cannot be Jewish just by *being*." That would be lapsing into the Gentile world. "So to remain Jewish is a *process*. . . " One of the temptations for Jews in the modern world is to live in the natural world (like the rabbi in "The Pagan Rabbi"), but Ozick argues that "What is holy is not natural, and what is natural is not holy." The Sabbath, for example, is a Jewish theological concept, a cultural integer, which is not natural but requires special human effort to obey.

> A Jewish literature is not a literature of wholeness; it too must have the angel's terrible mark left visibly in its sinew. Jewish literature, like a Jewish life, should leave us with the sense of having been struck in the very meat of our being, altered by the blow.[40]

Ozick's essays and stories often work through the same concepts albeit in different forms. In another essay, she states: "Literature does not spring from the urge to Esperanto but from the tribe."[41]

The particularity of Jews—of their history, their culture, and their destiny—remains Ozick's preoccupying theme. She criticizes liberal humanists who speak in universal terms when discussing the Holocaust. "Universalism is the ultimate Jewish parochialism,"[42] she states in one essay; in another, she expands upon this point:

> Now if being a Jew is being only what is universal, then a Jew is no more than his organs—no more than the dust of "dust unto dust"—and then what matter cremation?[43]

In disussing Auschwitz, she concludes:

> Blurring eases. Specificity pains. We have no right to seek a message of ease in Auschwitz, and it is moral ease to slide from the particular to the abstract.[44]

She goes on to remind her readers: "If we make an abstraction out of human wickedness...we will soon forget that every wickedness has had a habitation and a name."[45] Similarly, the Arab goal of the destruction of Israel cannot be viewed as anti-Zionist only but as fundamentally anti-Semitic. "If Israel burned, we here would turn into pillars and ash."[46] The destinies of all Jews, wherever they live, are intertwined, and the attackers of Israel are also the enemies of all Jews.

In a speech given at the America-Israel Dialogue in Rehovot, Israel in 1970, Ozick argued that the "American Exile" could become a creative center for Judaism. A new language, which she called "New Yiddish," combined with a new type of novel, the liturgical novel, could express Jewish themes within a vital moral sensibility. The Jewish novelist, using this new literary form "is in command of the reciprocal moral imagination rather than of the isolated lyrical imagination."[47] Jewish writers, immersed in Jewish tradition, could abandon the secular world forever. "When a Jew become a secular person he is no longer a Jew."[48] The opportunity, however, to reenter the holy world of Judaism does exist in America, the first diaspora existing simultaneously with the restoration and existence of the Jewish homeland. The questions of how and why this reentry would occur are not treated in Ozick's speech.

Ozick's essays are fiery and passionate. Her voice is an intense, committed one. It is reminiscent of the prophetic voices of earlier periods. Indeed, if Emma Goldman was a self-styled anarchist prophet, using the rhetoric and technique of Isaiah, Cynthia Ozick shares in the same tradition. Her fiction borrows story lines from the Jewish mystics as well as folklore; her essays decry the contemporary willingness to ignore the dangers facing modern Jewry. Most of Ozick's fictional characters are grappling with their Jewish heritage. They are knowledgeable, often deeply learned in the tradition, but their knowledge sometimes leads them astray. They are not beyond worldly temptation. Both Edelshtein and the character in "Usurpation" seek fame and fortune through their writing. Vanity remains a human frailty even among learned Jews.

In Ozick's universe, there are internal and external dangers facing Jews: the demons of the material world, of success, compete with the anti-Semites to see who will destroy the Jews first. The Jewish pagans yearn for union with the natural world and reject historical, contextual Judaism; the materialists pervert Jewish values and seek comfort, not justice; and in order to remind Jews that they remain the historical "other" in human history, the Arabs war against Israel. Ozick paints a picture of a turbulent, scarifying, and unpredictable world. Appropriate to her philosophy, her works all possess an unfinished quality to them, a sense of the never-ending process. Indeed, as long as Jews exist, write, and act as Jews, the story will not end. But to Ozick, in sharp contrast to many of the writers discussed, Jewish writers remain obligated to deal with their Jewishness rather than write in universalistic terms.

In a recent essay in *Lilith*,[49] the Jewish feminist magazine, Ozick confronts the feminist criticism of traditional Judaism. Writing in the style of a Talmudic exegesis in which the writer presents fifteen "meditations", with both supporting and refuting evidence for each position, she rejects the feminists' arguments. Ozick insists that the

Jewish view of women is based upon theology, not sociology.

> ...how trivializing it is to speak of the "influence" of the women's movement—as if Jewish steadfastness could be so easily buffeted by secular winds of power and pressure and new opinion and new perception. The truth is that it would be a blinding mistake to think that the issue of Jewish women's access to every branch and parcel of Jewish expression is mainly a question of "discrimination" (which, if that were all, *would* justify it as a feminist issue). No, the point is not that Jewish women want equality as women with men, but *as Jews with Jews.*[50]

Ultimately, Ozick departs from this position to argue that the Holocaust, with the terrible loss of so many Jews, necessitates the inclusion of women in the Torah-bound community as equals in order to perpetuate the Torah. The tortuous reasoning in this essay leaves the reader confused and bewildered. Women as women are not regarded as worthy of inclusion in the Jewish community, but rather as instruments to perpetuate a religious and cultural view that holds them in minimal regard. The writing of the essay, however, manifests Ozick's concern, and awareness, of the power of the feminist movement over Jewish women. If she did not see it as a threat, or a formidable critique of traditional Judaism, she would not have so responded.

Jewish American women writers of the twentieth century have shared many preoccupations although they have portrayed their subjects in unique ways. Intergenerational connections remains a major concern for all Jewish women writers. The relationship to religious Judaism, however, differs depending upon how close the writer is to the tradition. The third generation's interest in roots is evident in Jaffe's *Family Secrets* as well as in Parent's disparaging portraits. The question of who is responsible for the children's problems is answered through a critical look at the parents and the grandparents. Assimilation is not acknowledged as a problem in many of the contemporary women's fiction; there is no wish to retain a Jewish identity. Rather, the problem is in understanding the origins of the contemporary generation's neurosis.

While many Jewish women writers ignore the traditional dimension of Judaism altogether in their writings, Gail Parent mocks it. Edna Ferber finds the Yom Kippur service one of the most glorious and mysterious rituals she ever experienced. Anzia Yezierska criticizes

the scholarly father whose Judaism did not prevent him from op-
pressing his daughter. For Fannie Hurst, Thyra Samter Winslow,
and Grace Paley, the rabbi and the synagogue do not figure as vital
elements in their Jewish characters' lives. The Judaic content of
their stories rests in the characters, their world views, and their
personal dilemmas. Cynthia Ozick creates powerful, mystic rabbis
while Gail Parent satirizes the sterility of rabbis.

Contemporary Jewish women writers are also popular writers,
achieving fame reminiscent of Ferber and Hurst but for different
reasons. Ferber's heroines became Everywoman and her uplifting
American stories inspired readers. Hurst's melodramas touched the
hearts of many American women who had known sacrifice and suffering. In neither case were the female protagonists Jewish nor were
the women's plights uniquely associated with being Jewish in
America. In sharp contrast, the youngest generation of Jewish
American women writers, including Rona Jaffe and Gail Parent, portray Jewish "princes" and "princesses" as growing up culturally
disabled, as malfunctioning because of their Jewish background.

Grandparents, the representatives of the immigrant generation,
receive mixed treatment from these writers. To the native Jewish
women such as Winslow and Hurst, they represent a quaint, lovely
old tradition that is no longer appropriate to American life. To Paley
and Olsen, the grandparents represent a different tradition that is
equally irrelevant to modern life: socialism, Zionism, and Yiddish
appear as inappropriate philosophies for the children and grandchildren. Eva's humanism in *Tell Me a Riddle* is rejected by her
religiously observant children, and the Darwins' socialist-Zionist vision does not touch Faith Darwin. In *Family Secrets* Adam Saffron
has nothing to teach his progeny.

In the stories of Calisher and Paley, Jewish mothers and daughters
are engaged in serious human struggles, and are never portrayed
stereotypically. There are no "Jewish American princesses" in Grace
Paley's, Hortense Calisher's, or Cynthia Ozick's stories. There are no
Mrs. Portnoys until we get to the fiction of Jewish women writing in the
1970s. Gail Parent, in either imitation or parody of Philip Roth's
writings, creates caricatures of Jewish mothers. Although earlier
generations of Jewish women writers wrote disapprovingly of the ac-
quisitive Jew and the impressionable Jew, there was a note of sympathy for the immigrant's struggle and an understanding of the ir-
resistible temptations that confronted the first generation. The
dynamics of the conflict have been eliminated from much of the con-

temporary women's fiction about Jews. The characters become pasteboard figures who never debate assimilation versus the tradition or materialism versus idealism.

Mrs. Darwin, in Grace Paley's stories, is an independent mother striving to make her daughter into an independent woman; Faith Darwin has her problems but one of them is not being a "Jewish American princess." Calisher's Hester Elkin and her mother are engaged in a power struggle for affection. But in these exciting and excellent examples of imaginative treatments of a most important human theme, Judaism is neither blamed nor praised as the sole determining variable for the mother-daughter struggles, and none of the characters emerges as a caricature.

Among the Jewish American women writers, there are significant differences in philosophical priorities. Cynthia Ozick places her Judaism above her feminism; her fiction focuses on Jewish men, the traditional perpetuators of the scholarly tradition, rather than Jewish women. In Grace Paley's work, the problem of individual survival in a socially oriented and a secular moral universe, is emphasized rather than the issue of Jewish survival. For Hortense Calisher, individual understanding ranks high on the list of priorities, more so than survival. Cynthia Ozick is the only one of the group discussed who would tie individual and Jewish group survival together and argue that individual survival is meaningless without Jewish group survival. The integral role of Judaism in Ozick's vision places her apart from all of the other writers.

What is the relationship between fiction and reality? What do the portraits, the values, and the way of life of the imagination have to do with the historical reality of Jewish American women? I think there is an important, though not linear and equal, connection between the writer's world and the "real" world. The creative artist fashions her universe on the basis of personal and observed experience. She tries to join, in an exaggerated, dramatic, or understated manner, the truths of a specific human situation and the greater truths of life. If this assumption is correct, then the collective writing of Jewish American women writers, particularly the second and third generations, suggests that Jewish women are often bewildered, unsure of themselves, and unclear about the role of family, tradition, and religion in their lives.

7. Successful Mergers

Each of the previous discussions of the public lives of Jewish American women highlighted successful mergers between Judaism and American culture. Jewish women factory workers discovered a rude mixture of the two cultures. They had to adjust their commitments to Judaism to the realities of factory life. Their devotion to justice, to prophetic truths, and their optimism that the Judaic heritage could be realized in America made them union activists. To the Jewish women radicals like Emma Goldman and Rose Pastor Stokes, both cultures had to be transcended in order to create the humane culture they desired. The Jewish women volunteer activists successfully merged middle-class American and Jewish values; they acted within the respected role definitions for women in both the Jewish and American framework. As volunteers and community workers, they fulfilled everyone's idea of the proper role and behavior for Jewish American women. The Jewish women writers examined, sometimes critically, the existing merger. Their task was to make sense, both personally and socially, of the delicate interaction between Judaism and American culture.

This chapter focuses upon other varieties of synthesis, other examples from both the past and the present, of the public lives of Jewish women. In some cases, examples will be offered of Jewish women professionals who discussed the role Judaism played in their decision making, though their particular profession was not uniquely Jewish. In other instances, Jewish women chose professional work in Jewish institutions. The continued increase in the level of education of Jewish women and the economic affluence of growing numbers of Jews enabled families to educate their daughters along with their sons. This sociological fact plays a key role in the conspicuous presence of Jewish women among American women professionals.

Among the first generation of Jewish women who played public roles in America were the Yiddish actresses. Their resolution of the dilemma of how to integrate Judaism with American culture was to

ignore the American world as much as possible. As fervent Yiddishists, they were committed to preserving a language, a literature,
and a form of entertainment that were unique to Jews, wherever
they lived. A Yiddish actress playing Mirele in *Mirele Efros* knew
that she could play the same part in Yiddish theaters all over the
world; the goal of her public life was to retain and embrace the
Jewish culture, to maintain *Yiddishkeit*, in the American environment. Indeed, some of the actresses were tempted to the English-
speaking stage, some looked at the lights of Broadway and
temporarily abandoned the Yiddish stage for the Gentile audiences,
but most of the first generation remained loyal to the Yiddish theater
on the Lower East Side of New York and the Yiddish stages in all of
the cities with a significant Jewish population.

Yiddish actresses became idols in their community. The Jewish
women of the neighborhood emulated the fashions of the actresses
and attended their performances regularly. If actress Bertha
Kalisch wore a plumed hat, all of her fans promptly purchased the
same model. By 1918, a quarter of a million Jews attended the Yiddish theater regularly in New York City. One source lamented that,
in 1928, "nine out of ten Jews attend theatrical performances of Yiddish theater while not one out of ten attends synagogue."[1]

Born in Russia and trained in Europe, Keni Liptzen (1856–1918)
became the most famous Yiddish actress of the first generation. She
performed in most of the plays written by Jacob Gordin, the
acknowledged dean of the first generation of Yiddish playwrights.
One of Gordin's themes was "the need for women to become eman-
cipated in society."[2] Liptzen acted in Gordin's *Mirele Efros* in 1898,
when it was written, and made it a regular part of her repertory.
Because *Mirele Efros* became a standard part of the Yiddish-theater
repertory and featured a woman, a brief description of the plot is in
order.

Mirele Efros is the story of a widow by that name who is a very
successful businesswoman. She has two sons, to whom she is
devoted. Shalmon, her business associate, has been a faithful col-
league during the sixteen years she has been widowed. When the
play begins, Mirele is preparing to visit the family of her elder son's
fiancé. The family is not as wealthy as Mirele but they are pious people, a virtue important to traditional Jews. The visit does not prove
satisfactory as the bride's parents turn out to be greedy people, anxious to see their daughter Shaindell receive a generous dowry.
Mirele wants to break the marriage agreement but her son, Yosele,

pleads with her, declaring his love for Shaindell. Mirele relents and the marriage agreement is signed.

After the marriage, Shaindell becomes more and more demanding. She convinces her husband Yosele that he should manage the family business and that his mother's role should be diminished. Mirele decides to turn the business over to her sons—Yosele and the assimilated Donye, whose greed matches his sister-in-law's. Shalmon counsels Mirele to remain active in the business but she decides to please her son and daughter-in-law because, after all, who did she work so hard for if not her children? And if they are unhappy, then she cannot be happy. The decision turns out to be disastrous. Shaindell engineers the further estrangement of Yosele from his mother and Mirele, recognizing an intolerable situation when she sees one, leaves her house and lives elsewhere. She goes to work for Shalmon, who had been fired by Shaindell, and together they begin to build up another business, though Mirele will not compete with her son.

The years pass; Shaindell and Yosele have one son whom Mirele never sees. She mourns silently for her lost children. On the day of her grandson's Bar Mitzvah, his initiation ceremony into the adult community, Shaindell comes to see Mirele and plead with her to attend the Bar Mitzvah. Shaindell admits that Yosele has come to resent her interference in his life and she now realized that separating mother and son was wrong. Despite Shaindell's pleading, proud Mirele refuses her entreaties and says no. Shaindell leaves angry and heartbroken. As the day wears on, Mirele begins to regret her decision. She is then visited by her grandson Shloimele whose insistence finally wins her over. In the final scene of the play, Mirele goes to her son's house, her old house, and joins the Bar Mitzvah celebration. A family reconciliation is effected, and Mirele's final words are "Good children, bad children, but children after all." She raises her cup for the traditional Jewish toast: "To life." The curtain falls to cheering audiences and the women wipe their tears away, knowing that ungrateful children are most women's fate.

Mirele Efros was a popular part of the Yiddish-theater repertory for many years. The theme of a mother scorned by her children drew sympathetic responses in every audience. In 1939, the play was made into a movie starring Bertha Gerstein, another famous Yiddish actress of the time. The dignity of Mirele is effectively captured in Gerstein's portrayal. The eternal struggle of mother and son, parent and child, never ceased to intrigue theatergoers. Mirele emerges as a most admirable woman, a woman who tries to provide the best opportunities for her children and, when they turn against her, preserves her dignity and steps away from them. Mirele Efros is not a smothering mother; she gives up control over her sons, turns the business over to Yosele and gives him his independence. Shaindell, the daughter-in-law, emerges as the materialistic upstart who has lost whatever traditional values she once possessed. She displays no respect for her mother-in-law's wisdom or accomplishments, no interest in preserving family ties, and no compassion for the needs of others. She lives to regret her callousness, and so *Mirele Efros* ends with the classic happy ending: Justice is done and goodness prevails.

When the great Yiddish actresses are described, Bertha Kalisch's (1875-1939) name inevitably appears high on the list. The critic Alan Dale said of Kalisch, "... she is as good as Sarah Bernhardt at Sarah's best, but never as bad as Sarah at Sarah's worst."[3] Bertha Kalisch was born in Poland and trained for the opera in Europe. She came to New York in 1895 and starred in Gordin's Yiddish versions of *The Doll House* and Tolstoy's *The Kreutzer Sonata*. She was the first Yiddish actress to be lured to the English-speaking stage. A contemporary critic named Gorin prophesied that

> her leaving the Yiddish theatre, which robbed it of part of her repertoire, *Sappho* and *The Kreutzer Sonata*, was a portent of what would happen to the best strength of the Yiddish theatre which will be stolen away by the power of the American dollar[4].

An unnamed writer in the Yiddish press criticized the Yiddish audiences who enthusiastically welcomed Kalisch's return to the Yiddish stage (after her unsuccessful stint on Broadway). Kalisch defended her action by saying that she wanted to give the Yiddish theater a good name among the Gentiles.[5]

Celia Adler (1888-   ) was another well-known and well-regarded Yiddish actress. She was a member of a distinguished acting family; her father, Jacob Adler, was considered the dean of Yiddish actors. Celia, the offspring of Adler's marriage to his second wife Dinah Lipna, joined Maurice Schwartz's Yiddish Art Theater in 1919 and recruited other actresses such as Bertha Gerstein to that company. Celia's half-sister Stella and half-brother Luther (offspring of Adler's third marriage to actress Sarah Adler) joined Celia in the

Yiddish theater. In the 1930s, Stella Adler acted with the Group
Theater while Luther Adler became both a theatrical and movie ac-
tor.

Celia Adler was hired as a leading lady by Maurice Schwartz and
promised equal billing. Although she was a mature woman and a
mother in 1919, she played, according to Lifson,

> roles of a ten-to thirteen-year-old child. This was typical of most
> Yiddish theatre productions where children's roles, especially
> young boys, are played by mature, buxom women unconvincingly
> garbed as young people.[6]

Celia Adler became famous in many Perez Hirshbein plays. His *Far-
vorfen Vinkel, The Blacksmith's Daughter, Haunted Inn,* and *Green
Fields,* all Adler vehicles, also became the mainstay of Schwartz's
Yiddish Art Theater in the 1920s. Celia Adler also played in English
versions of Yiddish plays; most notably, she performed in the
Theatre Guild production of Pinski's *The Treasure.* In 1937, she starred
in the Yiddish film *Vu Iz Mayn Kind?* ("Where is My Child?")

Bertha Gerstein (1897-1976), who starred in the movie version of
Mirele Efros, was another star of the Yiddish theater. Celia Adler
convinced her to leave Boris Thomashevsky's National Theater and
join her at Maurice Schwartz's Yiddish Art Theater. Gerstein stayed
with the Schwartz company for twenty-five years. Born in Poland,
she had come to the United States in 1908 and played the Bar Mitzvah boy in *Mirele Efros* in her first Yiddish performance in this country. In the 1950s she was still acting; she appeared in the Broadway
production of *The World of Sholom Aleichem* in 1954 and in *A Majority of One* in 1959. A handsome woman, Gerstein had a dignified
and stately appearance that held her in good stead as Mirele;
however, when the Molly Goldberg image of the mature Jewish
woman took over in the 1950s, there was no market for the Gerstein
image.

Molly Picon (1898)-), a contemporary of Gerstein's, began in. the
Yiddish theater but made a successful transition to the Broadway
stage and the movies. She continues to be active and occasionally
can be seen in a movie. Until the 1940s, however, her acting took
place on Second Avenue at David Kessler's theater or on tour with
Yiddish plays. Molly Picon was an exception. Most of the generation
of Yiddish actresses born in the 1890s came of age during the
Golden Era of the Yiddish theater, the 1920s, and found it difficult, if

not impossible, to continue their acting career on the English speaking stage or in the movies. Many, having been born in Europe, had distinct accents, an unacceptable trait in the theater. Further, the acting techniques of the Yiddish theater encouraged exaggeration, emotional gestures, and hysterical outbursts. The English stage admired restraint, muted gestures, and underplaying a scene. The daughters of that generation, however, who sat on their parents' laps in the Yiddish theater, could become movie stars and dramatic actresses with ease. They benefitted from the rich exposure to the Yiddish theater but acquired none of its liabilities.

A third generation of Yiddish actresses was born in Europe in the 1910s and early 1920s and looked forward to a flourishing career in the rich Yiddish theater of Poland, Russia, Lithuania, and Latvia. Adolf Hitler dashed their hopes along with the lives of millions of Yiddish-speaking Jews. One member of that generation who fortunately came to New York in the fall of 1938 to perform at the Second Avenue Theater was Dina Halpern (1918-), a noted Warsaw actress whose aunt, Ester Rachel Kaminska, was considered the Sarah Bernhardt of Warsaw early in the century. It was at the Kaminska Yiddish Theater that Dina Halpern, along with her cousin Ida, learned the art of singing, dancing, and acting. Dina Halpern's uncle, Abram Halpern, was an impresario who managed her career in Poland. By the time she was twenty years old, Dina Halpern had toured Poland extensively and had performed in productions of plays by Hirshbein, Pinski, Gordin, and Sholom Aleichem. In 1937, she made two Yiddish movies, *The Dybbuk* and *The Vow*, which are still in circulation. In that same year, she appeared in *The Witch*, an Abraham Goldfadden play; this popular play had never had a woman act in the lead role before. In the 2,000-seat Nosvostye Theater in Warsaw, Dina Halpern played to sellout crowds for a whole year.[7]

In 1938, she accepted an eight-month contract at the Second Avenue Yiddish Theater in New York. At the end of the contractual period, Hitler's actions made a return to Poland impossible. Dina Halpern never saw her family again. She joined Maurice Schwartz's Yiddish Art Theater and starred opposite him in many productions including *It's Hard to Be a Jew* and *Shylock and His Daughter*. After the war, Dina Halpern toured all over the world doing Yiddish plays and recitals. Jewish communities in Europe, Canada, Argentina, Israel, and Australia welcomed her. While the Yiddish theater was on the wane in the post-World War II years in America, overseas

Jewish communities, made up largely of the survivors of European Jewry, made a conscious effort to preserve their Yiddish culture. It was to these audiences that Dina Halpern performed.

In 1948, while touring in Chicago with Maurice Schwartz, she met and married a theatrical publicist named Danny Newman. Chicago then became Dina Halpern's home. In 1949 and 1950, she appeared in two very successful Yiddish productions, *Anna Lucasta* and *The Little Foxes* at the sole remaining Yiddish theater in Chicago, The Douglas Park Theater. Both productions were great successes but they reflected the already changing tastes of Chicago Jewish audiences. Although performed in Yiddish, the plays were modern American dramas, not the products of the great Yiddish playwrights. In 1962, primarily because of the enthusiasm, talent, and energy of Dina Halpern and Danny Newman, the Yiddish Theater Association was established in Chicago; and from 1962 to 1970, the Association mounted seven productions for their Yiddish audiences.

The first, *Die Kishevmacher'n*, "The Witch," gave Dina Halpern the opportunity to perform in a role she had done in Warsaw thirty years earlier. For their 1963 production, Halpern chose the popular Sholom Aleichem comedy, *Dos Groise Gevins*, "The Grand Prize." *Mirele Efros* became the 1964 work while the twentieth-century Yiddish and Hebrew poet Kadya Molodowsky's *Donna Gracia Mendes* was the 1965 production. Molodowsky, a personal friend of Dina Halpern's and a leading Yiddish poet, featured in this play a strong and admirable woman. Donna Gracia was a sixteenth-century Marrano Jew in Antwerp who secretly observed Judaism in accordance with the last wishes of her brother-in-law, whose substantial estate she managed. Despite pressures from her sister, a devoted assimilationist, Donna Gracia remained committed to Judaism; as pressure from the Inquisition increased, she left Antwerp with her family, rejected a marriage offer from a French nobleman for herself and a marriage offer from the Prince of Aragon for her daughter, so that they could become openly practicing Jews in Turkey.

The remaining three productions, Sholom Aleichem's *Shver tzu Zein a Yid* ("It's Hard to Be a Jew,"), *Mishpachat Cahana* ("The Family Cahana"), and *The World of Itzhak Manger* were well received by the small but devoted audience of Yiddishists. But it became harder and harder to produce a Yiddish play. Although she was continually active as a recitalist, Dina Halpern had few opportunities in the late 1970s to act in Yiddish theater. Her dilemma is a sad but ac-

curate reflection of the decline of the once vibrant Yiddish theater
in America. But there are glimmers of interest in Yiddish. Yiddish-
speaking Jews in Winnipeg, Toronto, and Montreal as well as in
Sydney, Australia continue to produce amateur and semiprofes-
sional theatrical performances of Yiddish plays. Yiddish as a
language and a literature received new attention from the younger
generation in the late 1970s. It is not entirely unrealistic to predict
that the future will hold new, vital productions of Yiddish plays and
Dina Halpern will be only too glad to star as Mirele, the Witch, Donna
Gracia or a myriad of other favored roles.

Among the first generation of Jewish women who had ambitions to
perform on the stage were two women who chose burlesque and
vaudeville rather than the Yiddish theater. Sophie Tucker
(1887–1966) knew Yiddish actors as deadbeats who never paid their
restaurant and hotel bills. Working in her father's restaurant in
Hartford, Connecticut, she saw the touring Yiddish companies as
unreliable and less than successful. Although very ambitious and
desirous of a career in show business, she resolved to do it on the
American stage, not the Yiddish stage.[8] But Tucker's fluency in Yiddish and her proud identification as a Jew allowed her to integrate
Yiddish words, phrases, and intonations into her popular songs. Her
rendition of "My Yiddishe Mama" became a mainstay of her
nightclub act, an act that she perfected and performed for over fifty
years.

Although one critic called her voice "the voice with a stucco
finish," audiences loved her. Tucker spent years touring on the
vaudeville circuit, sharing the grueling life with many Jewish
cohorts who came from the same immigrant background as she did.
She later recalled:

> We all sprang from the same source, the same origin. We were all
> swept to the shores of this country on the same tidal wave of im-
> migration, in the same flight from prejudice and persecution. Our
> life stories are pretty much the same.[9]

By 1915, Sophie Tucker was billed at the top of the Palace Theater
marquee. Her act, which consisted of songs and stories, was given in
both Yiddish and English. Her rendition of "My Yiddishe Mama"
and her theme song, "Some of These Days," became famous and
were recorded for her growing audience. As late as the 1930s, her
Jewish audiences requested "My Yiddishe Mamma;" in a perfor-

mance in the East End of London in 1934, while she was singing this song, a group of Black Shirts booed her and when she was leaving the theater they threw stones at her. London newspapers registered numerous statements of indignation and Sophie Tucker returned a few years later to a triumphant engagement in London.[10]

Fanny Brice (1891–1951) was born and raised in New York within a Jewish environment but never knew Yiddish. Her natural singing voice led her to amateur night at the Keeney Theater in Brooklyn when she was fourteen years old. She won the audience's approval and became a regular at amateur nights throughout Brooklyn. She earned upwards of $70 a week as an amateur. It was Irving Berlin who suggested, in 1909, that she develop a Yiddish accent in her rendition of his song "Sadie Salome Go Home," and later in his "Goodbye, Becky Cohen." Fanny Brice took Berlin's advice and Sadie Salome became her trademark. She later recorded other Jewish ethnic songs such as "Becky Is Back in the Ballet," "Mrs. Cohen at the Beach," "The Song of the Sewing Machine," and "Oy How I Hate That Fellow Nathan."[11]

Brice's first song for the Ziegfeld Follies in 1910 was "I'm An Indian." Dressed in an appropriate Indian costume, she sang the song with a Yiddish accent and asked her audience: How could I tell my people that little Rosie Rosenstein was a little Indian girl? The mixing of genres, the American Indian/Yiddish girl combination, became the trademark of Fanny Brice's Ziegfeld Follies performances. Audiences loved her Yiddish intonations, her facial gestures, and her pose as the victim overcome by faithless lovers. Brice's humor was based upon the theme of vulnerability. As she told her biographer,

> In anything Jewish I ever did, I wasn't standing apart, making fun of the race. I *was* the race, and what happened to me on the stage is what could hapen to them. They identified with me, and then it was all right to get a laugh, because they were laughing at me as well as at themselves.[12]

Both Fanny Brice and Sophie Tucker found American entertainment congenial to their talents; both were able to retain their personal identification as Jews while performing red-hot-mama songs, comic routines, and blues ballads that appealed to all Americans. Just as their contemporaries Al Jolson and Eddie Cantor preserved their Jewish identification while linking their images to all Americans, so Brice and Tucker successfully used American forms and Jewish and American themes to become popular stars. Their particular pose and interpretations of human problems reflected their Jewish upbringing while the universal message of their work appealed to all Americans. As children of immigrants and having grown up in Jewish neighborhoods, they shared, with their audiences, a perspective and an identity.

Ethnicity was a vital and conscious factor for early-twentieth-century Americans. After all, the huge influx of Jewish, Italian, Russian, Polish, and other immigrants was a visible reality in all urban areas. Thus, entertainers of each ethnic group appealed to their own members, used material from their own cultural experience, and publicly built upon their origins. For entertainers who want the largest possible following, ethnic origins pose a problem: will they be limiting their appeal by basing too much of their routine on their ethnicity? The Jewish actors who became movie actors often resolved the dilemma by changing their names and eliminating all references to their Jewishness. With the recent revival of ethnicity as a positive value, entertainers can publicly acknowledge their cultural ties, if they still exist.

Few Jewish women, or any other group of women for that matter, participate in the public sphere as entertainers. More Jewish women entered the world, and created successful mergers, through traditional female occupations. Jewish women, beginning early in the century, took advantage of the American public-education system by attending school. With rising education, these women raised their hopes and expectations for work. They became teachers, nurses, and social workers, the agreed-upon female professions in America. Some Jewish women taught in the religious schools, a direct example of their commitment to Judaism. Most became public-school teachers and practiced their Judaism in the privacy of their home. There was no conflict between their public role and private life.

Jewish women, like most American women, chose occupations that harmonized with their primary role as wives and mothers. American society, indeed, did not encourage or allow women to pursue professions that endangered their domestic role. Few medical schools or law schools welcomed women and only a few brave women (until the late 1960s) dared to venture into public occupations that challenged traditional sex roles. Jewish women were no exception. They obeyed both the American and Judaic rule that a woman's major obligation was to her family.

When Ruth Sapinsky attended Wellesley College from 1906 to 1910, she was among a distinct minority. The major reason, she said, was:

> ...the majority of Jewish fathers and mothers are loath to permit their daughters to attend colleges at a distance when for approximately four years these daughters are divorced from family and friends and where, the parent fears, they learn habits of liberty and independence not at all compatible with a future of wifehood, motherhood, and domesticity.[13]

Although Sapinsky's explanation surely touched upon one vital factor, it ignored another: the very real economic hardship that the immigrant families faced. If parents were able to save some money, and children were able to work, the boy children would be sent to college, not the girl children. Daughters were expected to work and contribute to the family income while sons could use their earnings for themselves.

Writer Ruth Sapinsky (later Sapin) represented the exception for Jewish women in the early part of the twentieth century, not the rule. Born and reared in New Albany, Indiana, she found Wellesley intellectually and socially exciting though not without its problems, as Jewish girls were a distinct minority (3.2% of Wellesley's population). While attending the exclusive girls' college, she publicly argued that Jewish girls were not discriminated against, but in her reminiscence forty years later, she admitted that "no matter what their popularity or ability, Jewesses were never elected to high office either in class or general student organizations."[14] Based on imperfect sources, it appears that no more than 1,000 Jewish women attended college during 1915.

As Jewish families achieved middle-class status in America, they viewed college attendance for their daughters differently. By the 1950s, for example, Jewish parents considered college a possible marriage market for their daughters, a more desirable arena in which young women could find eligible mates. This is not to say that many Jewish women were not seriously interested in intellectual pursuits and in becoming teachers or social workers, but the added advantage of meeting a college man was not overlooked. Further, pragmatic Jewish parents reminded themselves, and their daughters, that an advanced education was a form of security in the event that as women they might someday have to support themselves or a family. In a 1957 Census Bureau study, it was reported that ten percent of Jewish American women had college degrees and 22.5 percent had had some college training.[15]

By 1971, over twenty-three percent of Jewish women workers were professionals in contrast to around fifteen percent of all American women.[16] This fact reflected the increased educational accomplishments of Jewish women. By the late 1960s, Jewish women were going to college in equal numbers with Jewish men, the first time in the history of the Jewish American experience that this had been the case. According to the 1971 National Jewish Population Study, 14.2 percent of Jewish women over twenty-five were college graduates; in 1975 it was found that, in the 25–29 age bracket, 23.2 percent of Jewish women were college graduates in contrast to only 13.9 percent of all white American women.[17]

What may have begun as family willingness to allow marriage-age daughters to attend college became, especially since the rise of the women's movement, a more self-conscious commitment on the part of the young women themselves to seek self-fulfillment. The American promise of education as a means of social and economic mobility, as the path to self-development, and as the key to human happiness surely merged in the minds of Jewish women with the age-old Judaic respect for learning. In America, Jewish women achieved the educational opportunities given to Jewish men throughout history.

An early example of a Jewish woman educator in America was Julia Richman (1855–1912). Indeed, Richman qualifies as part of the minority, the extremely few American women in the late nineteenth century who became full-time careerists. Richman, a native New Yorker, was born to Bohemian Jewish immigrant parents and educated at Normal College (later Hunter College). In 1872, she became a New York City teacher and then in 1884, a principal of Public School 77 for nineteen years. In 1903, she became the first Jewish woman district superintendent in the New York City school system.

Julia Richman was proud of her Jewishness and was deeply committed to education as an essential tool for all people. She combined her interests by helping the growing numbers of Jewish immigrants to this country through her work with the Educational Alliance in the 1880s and 1890s, by participating in the activities of the National Council of Jewish Women, and by being the first president of the Young Women's Hebrew Association. Richman believed that flexible educational programs could aid Jewish immigrants in their adjustment to America. At the same time, she wanted to preserve Jewish identity and culture. She worked with the religious school of her temple and devised courses for moral education.

Julia Richman used the social-work approach and the settlement-house model for her work in the New York City schools.[18] She was a friend of Lillian Wald, the founder of the Henry Street Settlement House, and admired Wald's visiting-nurses program for the immigrant tenants on the Lower East Side of New York. When she became a district superintendent, Richman had a choice of any school district in the city. She chose the Lower East Side of New York, the neighborhood known jointly as "Little Italy" and "Little Israel," because, as her sisters noted, "the tremendous influx of immigrants had brought problems there which no other section of the city faced."[19]

Richman had been active as a teacher and board member of Reform religious schools in New York for many years. She observed the inadequate instruction, the volunteer teachers, and the large classes. In an effort to improve the situation, she wrote half of a correspondence course for religious-school teachers entitled "Methods of Teaching Jewish Ethics," participated in the publishing of a monthly magazine for Jewish religious schools called *Helpful Thoughts*, and lectured frequently on the problems of religious education. In her role as district superintendent, she often coordinated her public schools' activities with the Americanization work of the Educational Alliance.[20]

Julia Richman believed in a blending of the Judaic tradition with American law and custom. She criticized the Jewish peddlers who worked on Sundays, in defiance of the laws, who sold goods without a license, and who refused to speak English. In 1908, as a result of her strict position and inflexible stance, a petition circulated on the Lower East Side to have Richman removed from her superintendency because of her unsympathetic attitude toward the immigrants. She was reprimanded in the petition for "reviling and maligning the inhabitants of the East Side...." Because of her support from influential Jews such as Louis Marshall and Board of Education member Felix Warburg, the petition failed to effect any change.[21]

Julia Richman cared deeply about immigrant children and the preservation of Judaism. However, she believed that adaptation to the new environment was essential. Immigrant children should learn English and job skills. Orthodox Jews should mold their religious beliefs to the American setting. As she once put it:

> In this country we are not Jews first and Americans afterwards; we are American Jews, imbibing loyalty to our country in our American schools...and drawing our Jewish sentiment from family tradition and congregational life.[22]

Richman retired as superintendent in 1912, at the age of fifty-six. She planned on writing and lecturing after a summer vacation in Europe. Unfortunately, her plans were thwarted when she became ill on the ship crossing the Atlantic and died in Europe of complications following an appendectomy. In one of the many eulogies written after her death, an *American Hebrew* editorial captured her continued interest in both the Jewish community as well as education for all.

> As for her Jewish interests, it may be said that she gave her best efforts to the application of her experiences and talents as a teacher to Jewish educational problems in New York, as well as to other phases of Jewish educational activity in the country at large.... She believed in education that had pragmatic value, and she was deeply concerned for the religious and moral education of the patrons of the institution. Her position in the public-school system enabled her to use her experiences there for the betterment of the Alliance, which fortified her in her work as district superintendent.[23]

As both a Jew and an American, Julia Richman believed that education was a necessary tool to becoming a moral human being and an effective member of society. Education provided both the intellectual and economic tools to succeed in society. She devoted her professional career to realizing that principle. A high school in Manhattan was named for Julia Richman after her death, and many Jewish women followed her lead by attending Hunter College and becoming public-school teachers and administrators.

Some Jewish women became teachers in the religious and Hebrew schools of synagogues. One of the paradoxes of Judaism is its commitment to education but low regard for educating as a profession. Jewish men become the principals and administrators within the

Jewish educational system (as they do in secular schools), but much fewer can be found in the classroom. In a survey of Jewish administrators, one anonymous commentator has observed: "The long-standing tradition of an all male rabbinate often militates against the appointment of women to many senior educational posts."[24] The remembrance of women as volunteers in all temple functions also plays a role. Males are professionals and women are volunteers. The male as authority figure prevails in most administrative and leadership roles in the synagogue, though there was evidence in the late 1970s of changes in this area. The Jewish women teachers in America's public schools and colleges have fulfilled their individual and cultural interest in education, while the Jewish women teachers in Jewish religious schools demonstrate their specific commitment to Jewish survival by channelling their educational aims in this direction.

The field of Jewish education poses special problems for women professionals. Most of the teachers in Hebrew and religious schools are not graduates of a college of Judaica. Many have taken courses in the field and are certified secular teachers, but rarely are they specialists in Jewish studies. Part of the reason for this is that the work is not full-time; Hebrew schools meet in the afternoon after public school and on Sunday mornings. Sometimes the teachers hold teaching positions in the public schools or are parents interested in a part-time commitment to Jewish education. The synagogual authority is the rabbi, who until very recently was always a male, and the principal of the Hebrew and religious school has similarly always been male. To include women in the ranks of administrators in the male-dominated synagogue will require a major value change in Judaism, one that Reform and Conservative Judaism are beginning to make.

Social work has occupied the talents of many Jewish women professionals since the 1910s. Esther Loeb Kohn and her generation of volunteer settlement-house workers have been replaced by college-educated social workers. The various organizations and community centers created by the Jewish community and every other community to serve its people became the laboratories and the field-study centers for the new schools of social work. As the government became more involved in the business of social welfare, the number of social-welfare institutions grew, as did the social-work profession. Within the Jewish community, social workers became the professionals who dealt with the patients in the Jewish hospitals and the clients at the family-service agencies. Community centers and homes for the aged also had their specially trained staff workers.

As early as 1899, the National Conference of Jewish Communal Service was organized; its creation reflected the existence of various Jewish professional groups and the need for overall coordination. In the 1970s, there are professional associations of Jewish Community Organization workers; Jewish Center workers; Jewish Family, Children's and Health Service personnel; Jewish Homes for the Aged personnel; Synagogue Administrators; and Jewish Vocational and Rehabilitation Services workers.[25]

One of the models for the social-welfare agency, of course, was the settlement house. And one of the most important woman founders was Lillian Wald (1867–1940).Wald, a Jewish nurse from Rochester, New York, started the Henry Street Settlement House as a volunteer facility in 1893 for Jewish immigrants on the Lower East Side. As a professional nurse, she used her special knowledge to begin a visiting-nurses program; she provided classes in prenatal care to the neighborhood women, and she taught nutrition to the mothers. Wald was a pragmatist who believed in utilizing her skill and knowledge to help a dependent group achieve independence. She assembled a professional staff of nurses and social workers to aid her in her task. Volunteers also played a crucial role at the Henry Street Settlement House.

Lillian Wald, a nurse and settlement-house leader, and Julia Richman, a professional educator, are an interesting pair of native Jewish American women from comfortable backgrounds who chose to devote their lives to others. Neither married and both remained dedicated to the immigrants who became their constituency, their life, and their hope. Both humanized the harsh surroundings of the Lower East Side for the Jewish immigrants during a trying period. Lillian Wald established the first outdoor playground in New York City and got a school lunch program underway. Julia Richman's work as a religious-school teacher and writer as well as her board activities with the Educational Alliance eased the path of adjustment for the immigrant and native Jewish children.

Wald and Richman were cultural Jews who associated with Jews, identified as Jews, but also operated successfully in the American secular environment. Richman shared her expertise with her temple's Sunday-school staff while Wald felt more comfortable in the Ethical Culture Society, a group committed to a humanistic philosophy. While Lillian Wald worked with immigrant East European Jews, her ethnic affiliation was with upper-class German Jews. Both Richman and Wald integrated aspects of both the Jewish and American cultures into their lives. They performed practical good works for needy Jews and applied their professional skill and knowledge to their compatriots. But socially and culturally, they lived in the secular American environment.

Although many Jewish American women entered the profession of social work, the only ones about whom we can learn are those who worked in Jewish social-service agencies and became active in the professional Jewish social-work organizations. Miriam R. Ephraim, for example, was elected president of the National Association of Jewish Center Workers in 1937, the first woman to hold that position since its creation twelve years before.[26] As of 1973, Miriam Ephraim was still active in the social-work field; she was secretary general of the International Conference of Jewish Communal Service.[27] With the growth of Jewish community centers in every community with a Jewish population, the need for professional workers grew; so did the concomitant need for a professional organization that shared information, provided a national forum, and called regular conferences to communicate common problems. According to one source, there were 1,000 members of the National Association of Jewish Center Workers in 1964.[28]

One of the unfortunate but predictable offshoots of professionalization in any field is the decrease in women's participation and the increase in men's entrenchment in the area. When medicine consisted largely of midwifery, women dominated. Once medical schools, formal exams, and long years of preparation became the requirement, women were excluded from the medical ranks. The educational structures were not shaped according to a woman's life and no efforts were made to accommodate young mothers or to encourage women to forestall marriage and motherhood in order to complete the additional years of study. Only as long as "on-the-job" training was allowed could women participate freely.

Even in "female" professions such as social work, men entered the field and became the high-status and high-paid administrators. In teaching, the same pattern prevailed: while the overwhelming majority of teachers are women (eight out of ten), the overwhelming majority of principals and superintendents are men. Only one of sixty-three superintendents is female.[29] In the area of Jewish social work, the same unpleasant phenomenon exists. In a 1975 study of women's opportunities in Jewish social work, it was noted that there were few women in executive directorships of Jewish community centers, homes for the aged, or synagogues.

Sara Feinstein, former Director of Jewish Education and Culture for the Jewish Federation of Chicago, conducted a survey of seven professional fields within the National Conference of Jewish Communal Service. The respondents generally agreed that women were reluctant to assert themselves; in the cases of the Jewish community centers and the vocational and rehabilitation services, the professions were traditionally male. In all of the fields surveyed, women were poorly represented in leadership positions.[30]

At their formation early in the century, the various Jewish family, children's, and health service agencies were headed by women; in the mid-1930s, when the first generation of women administrators began to retire, they were replaced by men. As long as the field was still new, it was acceptable for women to occupy positions of authority. Once the jobs achieved some status and prestige, men sought them and were chosen over women. The rationale given for the lack of women in directorships of the Jewish homes for the aged, until recently, was that women had not chosen health-administration specialties and few were qualified for executive positions in the field. The lack of women synagogue administrators was explained thus:

> For many years women were the backbone of volunteers in synagogue life, and it is difficult for them to be accepted as paid professionals because they still continue to do much work in the synagogue on a non-paid basis....[31]

It is truly ironic that the overwhelming image of the woman as volunteer has militated against accepting the woman as professional.

Despite this dilemma, the social reality is that more and more Jewish women are becoming professional workers. In fact, the Jewish woman professional is no longer only a single woman who works briefly before marriage, but a married woman with or without children. Her education as a social worker has also changed, with growing emphasis upon counseling skills and knowledge about geriatrics. Growing numbers of Jewish women social workers have Master's degrees with emphasis upon psychiatric social work. The Jewish community is growing older and more integrated into American society. The increase in single Jewish parents, the growing population of senior citizens, and the influx of Soviet Jews since 1976 have all created new social concerns for the professional and lay Jewish community.

Anna Moscowitz Kross is an excellent example of a rarity in the first generation, a Jewish woman lawyer, a professional, at a time when women lawyers were few in number. Kross combined her commitment to the Jewish community with her devotion to law. Born in 1891 in Neshves, Russia, she came to this country as an infant with her parents; she was the only one of the three Moscowitz children who survived the steerage passage across the ocean. Her parents were poor but supported her will to learn. Anna Moscowitz went to school during the day and worked in a factory at night to support herself. She received a scholarship to study law at night at New York University. When she received her law degree in 1910, she was too young to take the bar exam. She then obtained a Master's degree the following year. In 1912, she was admitted to the bar and became an investigator in women's court for a women's organization. For five years, while practicing law as well, she studied the corrupt conditions that prevailed in that court. Twenty years later, as a magistrate in women's court, she publicized the shady lawyers, corrupt policemen, and wily bailbondsmen who frequented its corridors. In 1917, she married Isidor Kross. The Krosses had three daughters, one of whom died during childhood.

During the course of a rich public career as lawyer, magistrate, and commissioner of corrections of New York City, Anna Moscowitz Kross spoke frequently before women's groups, and especially Jewish women's groups, on a variety of favorite themes: the need for women to be active in public affairs, the particular need of Jewish women to serve their community, and the requirement for justice to be administered scientifically and humanely. In 1934, she became cochairman of the building-fund committee for the New York chapter of Hadassah with the charge given to raise $200,000 for the Hadassah Hospital in Jerusalem. Her service in this capacity demonstrated Magistrate Kross's deep involvement in Hadassah and Zionism. As her work in women's court grew, she devoted more time to secular social issues; juvenile delinquency and improving the prisons of New York City became preoccupying concerns. Understandably, less time was given to specifically Jewish causes, but the frequent reporting of her speeches in the *New York Times* throughout the 1930s, 1940s, and 1950s demonstrates her active public-speaking career and her unwavering devotion to social justice.[32]

Anna Moscowitz Kross's public life is an impressive example of a woman who became successful in her chosen profession while maintaining an active involvement in Jewish women's communal organizations. In 1934 Hadassah honored her for her contributions to their organization as well as for her achievements as a magistrate. Her visibility in New York City provided at least two generations of New York City Jewish women with a role model of an able woman with a high energy level who was a wife, mother, judge, and social reformer. Magistrate Kross frequently spoke before the Business and Professional Women's Association and encouraged young women to pursue their own careers and to become public persons with identities of their own. In a speech before the Sisterhood of Congregation B'nai Jeshurun in 1934, entitled "A Fuller Participation of Women in Public Life," she told her audience that "it [was] necessary for women to go beyond the boundaries of their homes and enter public life and to interest themselves in civil and social service."[33]

In a career that spanned over fifty years (Kross retired as commissioner of corrections at the age of seventy-five in 1966), Anna Moscowitz Kross, who used her full name throughout her public career, acted as the voice for the downtrodden—for the prostitutes who were being victimized by officialdom, for juvenile delinquents who had no rehabilitative help, and for criminals who were mistreated in prisons. Over forty years ago, she told a reporter that "we now regard as social problems many deviations of human conduct that were considered crimes a generation ago."[34] Her persistent theme, in all of her crusades for justice, was righteous treatment of vulnerble people, a principle articulated by the prophets over 2,000 years ago. In the American community, Anna Moscowitz Kross, like Deborah the judge in ancient times, worked to translate abstract concepts of law into living realities for people. In a letter to the *New York Times* in 1964, she summed up her work in this way:

I have spent practically the whole of my adult life in the struggle to raise the status of woman to that of man before the law of our land in every respect—but, as you know, there is still a great distance to go. Even when the law permits, custom frequently does not.[35]

Perhaps the best prospect of a successful merger lies in the growing interest of young Jewish women in becoming rabbis. The rabbinic profession enables a man or a woman to combine scholarly, religious, personal, and social pursuits. The fact that Jewish women have begun to suggest that this most traditionally male Jewish occupation should be opened up to them reflects recent American social trends. As one commentator on the subject noted: "The national women's liberation movement and the Jewish feminist movement have already contributed to changes in the way Jewish women perceive themselves and their roles in Jewish life."[36] The term "Jewish feminists," commonly used in the 1970s, accurately denoted the juxtaposition of the contemporary women's movement and Judaism. Jewish women began examining their religion from a feminist perspective, and the occupation that epitomized Jewish scholarship and leadership became the target for some Jewish feminists.

In 1972, Sally Preisand became the first woman to be ordained. By the end of the decade, twenty-three women had been ordained by the faculty of the Hebrew Union College-Jewish Institute of Religion. By 1980, within the Reform movement, women constituted nearly thirty-three percent of the student body of the rabbinical school.[37] By 1979, four women had become rabbis within the Reconstructionist movement, and two women at the liberal Leo Baeck School in London were ordained.[38] At the Hebrew Union College's School of Music in Cincinnati in 1977, seventeen women, out of forty-four students, were studying to become cantors.[39]

While the Orthodox Jewish movement does not even countenance discussions of the subject, the Conservative movement has been considering the ordination of women as rabbis since 1977. Chancellor Gerson T. Cohen of the Jewish Theological Seminary created a commission to study the subject; the final report, submitted in December 1978, recommended positive action.[40] But the faculty of the Seminary tabled the matter in a highly emotional and controversial debate on the issue in December 1979. However, the matter remained volatile. In May 1980, the Rabbinical Assembly of the Conservative movement, composed of the majority of Conservative rabbis in the United States, voted (156-115) a resolution favoring the ordination of women as rabbis.[41]

Moment magazine polled its readers on this subject in the spring of 1980.[42] Six hundred people responded, with sixty-six percent very much in favor of women's ordination. When the sample was broken down according to religious affiliation, the following statistics emerged:

Reform Jews:	79%	very much in favor
	16%	somewhat in favor
	95%	favorably disposed
Conservative Jews:	57%	very much in favor
	22%	somewhat in favor
	79%	favorably disposed
Orthodox Jews	19%	very much in favor
(fewest respondents):	12%	somewhat in favor
	31%	favorably disposed
	56%	against ordination of women

Although this sample was by no means representative or comprehensive, it reveals something of the contemporary sentiments on the subject. When divided according to sex, more women predictably favored the idea than men: seventy-five percent of the women favored the idea as opposed to fifty-six percent of the men.

The issue of women rabbis symbolized the drastic changes in modern consciousness. Supporters credited, and critics blamed, the women's movement for its role in encouraging or instigating Jewish women to consider issues that had been previously unexplored. Although, in one recent research survey of Orthodox Jewish women who combined careers with marriage, it was noted that there were strains in the family, eighteen of the women interviewed said that "women's liberation made them feel better about their professional roles and lessened guilt over leaving children to fulfill themselves."[43] The fact that religiously orthodox women acknowledged the influence of the women's movement upon their attitudes and behavior dramatically exemplifies how far-reaching the contemporary women's movement has been. No group of Jewish women were immune to its message. This is not to say that all Jewish women became feminists, but that even the most zealously orthodox were required to reexamine their reasons for their particular beliefs and either modify them to accommodate the new possibilities, or at least acknowledge the existence of other philosophical positions.

Rabbi Samuel Joseph, who in his capacity as National Director of

Admissions for the Hebrew Union College visited forty-one college campuses during the 1979–1980 academic year, has concluded that there would be a continued increase in women's enrollment at the rabbinic seminary.[44] The numbers of women rabbis and of women rabbinical students, of course, are still so few as to make predictions about future possibilities very difficult. Women rabbis may be the beginning of a new social type, or they may remain a visible but distinct minority of women who defy custom and tradition but do not necessarily mark out a new professional path for Jewish women.

Many variables come together to create a woman professional, especially a Jewish woman professional; they are sometimes difficult to identify and label with certainty. Phyllis Chesler, a noted American psychologist of today who has written the best-selling book *Women and Madness*, considers her professional interest in women and their mental health to be based upon her Jewish identity. Indeed, she has noted in a recent interview that Judaism was probably the source for her feminism as well.

> The reason I am a feminist has very much to do with the passion for justice and the irrational belief that reason can prevail, that I learned as a Jew.[45]

Chesler described her upbringing as Orthodox; she studied Hebrew, was a member of Hashomer Hatzair, a Socialist-Zionist group, and thought that she would become a rabbi when she grew up. The fact that she could not study like the boys and prepare for a Bar (or Bat) Mitzvah made her abandon her plans and seek elsewhere for intellectual and psychic stimulation. It was not until she had become a psychologist and an articulate feminist that she rediscovered her Jewish roots. Many of the women in the feminist movement defined her as a Jewish feminist, she recalled, and this recognition made her reassert the identity she then claimed proudly.

Chesler considered herself a Zionist, began wearing Jewish stars to feminist rallies, and believed that her Judaism, Zionism, feminism, and socialism were all compatible philosophies, belief systems that had traditionally been embraced by Jews. Although traditional Jewish texts do not treat women in the feminist ways she would like, she is able to glean much wisdom from them nonetheless.

When I read the *Chumash* as a feminist, I can tear my hair and put ashes on my head. When I read it as Jew, I always learn from it.

> The value placed on books, on education, on literature is a Jewish value, brought about mostly by exile and persecution. The hope that revolution can take place through education, through the use of the mind, is a Jewish value.[46]

Phyllis Chesler's intellectual proclivities led her to psychology as a profession and to Zionism, socialism, and feminism as a philosophy. She has created a successful merger of these ideologies in her mind; as such, she provides an exciting role model for other Jewish women who wish to retain their Jewish identity, become feminists, and pursue a professional career. Indeed, this may be the model for the Jewish woman professional of the future: a Jewish woman whose heritage is known to her and who expresses it through her particular profession. Her devotion to intellectuality, to social causes, and to integrating her Jewish and American identities into a cohesive whole become the new definition of a Jewish woman professional for the last part of the twentieth century.

Some successful contemporary Jewish women professionals remember childhood readings about Jewish women leaders that influenced them. Cynthia Fuchs Epstein, a successful sociologist today, has described the influence Jewish women role models had upon her own ambitions:

> I never imagined that by my own mind or hands I could achieve the exalted position to which I aspired. This was in spite of the fact that my father liberally bestowed on me books containing the biographies of great women, particularly great Jewish women: Deborah in the Bible, the poet Emma Lazarus whose poem is engraved on the Statue of Liberty, and the socialist Rosa Luxemburg. I suppose these had impact, however, because they exposed me to the idea that women could be doers and movers although I was terribly insecure about my own competence to move or do anything.[47]

Epstein, in searching for the reasons for her own success despite an insecure self-image, recognized the role played by Jewish women achievers of the past. Indeed, one does not need to read about a Jewish woman doctor in order to decide to become a doctor.

The transference and the emulation do not have to be direct or explicit; rather, the model of an accomplished Jewish woman inspires the reader to attain her own professional goal.

Notwithstanding these positive connections between Judaism and women as professionals, there are also notable obstacles to the Jewish woman's self-development as a professional. Scholarship and achievement outside the home have largely been male domains. Both in the past and the present, powerful cultural forces militate against women becoming professionals. It was the extraordinary parents who encouraged their daughters to become professionals. In 1910, it was the bold daughter who defied convention and her parents' wishes to become a professional worker. Paradoxically, while the Jewish culture did not encourage women to become professionals, it often recognized their accomplishments when they did so. Jewish magazines and newspapers in this country frequently noted the good work of a Jewish woman lawyer, actress, or doctor. The Jewish community took pride in the accomplishments of their own, whether they were male or female Jews.

One popular Jewish woman politician, who knowingly or unknowingly shares a tradition with the Jewish radical women of the early twentieth century, is Bella Abzug. A member of the House of Representatives from 1970 to 1976, Abzug discusses her Jewish heritage freely and proudly. She speaks frequently before Jewish women's groups and interrelates her Jewish and feminist themes. At the age of eleven, Bella Abzug spoke in the subway stations of New York on behalf of Zionism. She studied at the Jewish Theological Seminary of America and Hunter College before going to Columbia University Law School. To be socially concerned and to be Jewish are not only compatible states for Bella Abzug; they are inextricably related.

Zionism, socialism, and feminism provide the ideological guidelines for Abzug's activism. As a lawyer and a congresswoman she was able to act constructively on behalf of these beliefs. As a legislator, she was an articulate spokeswoman for Israel, for women's rights, and for civil rights for all Americans. She supported social-welfare programs for the poor, the disadvantaged, and the minorities of America. Working simultaneously for Israel and for the deprived of America was entirely compatible with her philosophy. Indeed, Bella Abzug's view of social justice as founded upon Judaism but applicable to all human beings allows her to speak for all of the downtrodden while remaining irrevocably Jewish. It is interesting to see the merging of so many traditions in the life and career of Bella Abzug. She appears as a natural outcome of being Jewish, an independent woman, and a bright American simultaneously.

With Jewish women obtaining the same advanced education as their brothers in the 1970s and 1980s, it is very likely that the number of Jewish women professionals will continue to rise. Although they will generally follow the traditional female professions such as teaching and social work, more and more (like more and more American women in general) will become doctors, lawyers, scientists, and engineers. The psychic support of the women's movement combined with a Judaic culture that respects learning and accomplishment will encourage more and more Jewish women to achieve intellectually and professionally. The tension between family and career, however, will also continue as there is no simple answer to this problem. The high value placed upon family in the Jewish tradition will be felt as will the individual's wish to achieve. More and more Jewish women will return to college and graduate school after their families are raised, a phenomenon occurring for women in general in America today.

While Jewish women professionals will practice their professions both within the Jewish community and in the larger American society, many Jewish volunteer activists will continue their public lives within the Jewish community. Contemporary Jewish women entertainers, in contrast, have generally lost their connection with Judaism. That is, their Jewish identification and Jewish commitment no longer play a role in their public lives as performers. The Yiddish actresses have lost their stage or a viable audience, and Fanny Brice has been replaced by Barbra Streisand, who, indeed, recreated Brice's life on the stage and on film, but displays no connection to her Jewish origins in her public work.

Jewish women writers will continue to wrestle with the meaning of their self-definition and of the positive and negative aspects of their Jewish heritages; for good or ill, the Jewish component of their family and communal upbringing will concern them. If Judaism loses its hold, then the synthesis will fade and the sole cultural influence will be the American one. Successful mergers will only be made by Jewish American women for whom both parts of the equation remain vital.

8. Future Directions

The recent past provides us with a backdrop for the future. Jewish women on American college campuses in the 1960s and 1970s are becoming the adult generation, the leadership generation, for the remainder of the century. Their participation in all of the social-protest movements that characterized campus life in the 1960s and early 1970s surely has and will influence their postcollege behavior. Many have become leaders and followers in the women's liberation movement while others, especially after the Arab-Israeli War of 1967, have become fervent Zionists, anxious to learn about their history and interested in reforging links to their Jewish heritage. In the late 1970s, there was evidence of a new interest among younger Jewish women in Hadassah and other Jewish women's organizations. Membership among newly married women, single women professionals, and college-age students was on the rise.[1]

Jewish youth, male and female, played a major role in college-campus activism in the 1960s.[2] One source claimed that twenty percent of the students in the Free Speech Movement at Berkeley in 1964 were Jewish.[3] Sociologist Richard Flacks has reported that forty-five percent of the University of Chicago students who participated in the Selective Service System sit-in in 1966 were Jewish.[4] Sociologist Nathan Glazer argued in an interesting essay called "The New Left and the Jews" that the Jewish youth in the New Left in contrast to their parents and ancestors who peopled the Old Left, had no cultural foundation in Judaism, and that they shared the anti-Israel and anti-Semitic rhetoric and philosophy of their Gentile friends.

It is impossible to determine how many of the Jewish New Left broke with their politically radical friends and became Zionists, feminists, or moderate liberals. Follow-up studies of college radicals suggest at least three possible routes: making a professional commitment to social-justice causes; dropping out of social activism; and retreating into middle-class, self-fulfilling professionalism. Phyllis Chesler, whom we have already discussed as an example of a successful merger of Judaism and feminism, surely qualifies as an example of the first and third types. She is a successful psychologist as well as a spokeswoman for women's rights. Elizabeth Holtzman, a Congresswoman from Flatbush since 1972, typifies the professionally able woman who channels her commitment to social justice through the legislative process. She is a culturally comfortable Jew who neither proclaims nor denies her Jewish identity. She supports Israel and speaks out against any overt anti-Semitic references; Holtzman has also been instrumental in getting the Justice Department to prosecute Nazis in the United States. She received her education during the turbulent sixties at Radcliffe and Harvard Law School but focused upon her own personal and professional development.

The most extreme example of an Orthodox Jewish woman whose involvement with radical feminism led to her break with Orthodoxy was Shulamith Firestone. Her book the *Dialectics of Sex* (1971) is a devastating critique of capitalism and Western culture. Firestone's thesis is that there is no possibility for respectful human contact between men and women in this society and test-tube babies (which she discussed before the technology had been perfected) should be the only method to create a next generation. Her total disillusionment with religious orthodoxy and Western society in general marks the most complete example of how a sensitive and politically involved woman responds to radical protest movements during her formative years.

The college-educated Jewish women of the 1960s and 1970s went on to graduate school, marriage, and career. They differed from their mothers in the level of education and professional training that they acquired, but they displayed little public activism. Their sisters, a decade or less younger, may have joined Zionist clubs or college campuses but generally, true to the "me-ism" of the American culture of the 1970s concentrated on their own studies and postponed worrying about the merger of their Jewishness, their individuality, and their personal ambition.

The women's liberation movement gave Jewish women one set of questions and answers to consider while the upsurge of Zionism made them examine their commitment to Israel. Those women raised in traditional Jewish homes had to reconcile their second-class status in the synagogue with their newfound feminism and their awareness of current social-change movements. Many tried to create a new harmony out of feminism, Judaism, and Zionism. Others who were committed to Marxism found the philosophic parts even harder to meld. Some abandoned all but one of these ideologies and declared their unilateral support for feminism, socialism, or Zionism. There has not been one prevailing pattern, but rather a variety of responses.

Some Jewish women who are committed to Judaic practices have tried to synthesize Judaism with feminism. They founded consciousness-raising groups and have tried to harmonize their dual loyalties. Judith Plaskow, for example, said at the National Jewish Women's Conference in New York City in February 1973:

> We are here because a secular movement for the liberation of women has made it imperative that we raise certain Jewish issues now, because we will not let ourselves be defined as Jewish women in ways in which we cannot allow ourselves to be defined as women.[5]

Feminism preceded Judaism in Plaskow's priorities. In order to achieve a harmony between the two philosophies, some women have proposed an alteration in traditional synagogual practices and have recommended the inclusion of women in the *minyan*, the allowance of women to read from the Torah, and the elevation of the Bat Mitzvah to equal status with the Bar Mitzvah. Reform Jewish temples, and some Conservative synagogues, have already responded to the new feminist concern and allow women to read from the Torah and to be included in the *minyan*. Orthodox Jewry has not yielded on any of these points.

One Jewish women's group in New York devised a Jewish women's prayer to replace the male prayer in the morning service (which blessed God for not making them women). It reads:

> Blessed are you, our God, who put the world in order, and who is the Creator of our Mothers. I am awed by the cycles of life that are like the moon in her path. Blessed are you, my God, who has created me a woman.[6]

The Jewish women's rebellion of the 1970s is different from the radicalism of the early twentieth century in that it is more diverse. Jewish women rebels today may choose to remain traditional Jews but try to reform Judaism from within. This position never received public attention in previous periods. Although Rosa Sonneschein criticized Jewish women's lack of status in synagogual affairs in the 1890s, she never reached a significant audience nor did she enlist many women supporters to her cause. Today, Jewish feminist groups can be found in every major city with a Jewish population. Zionism, only a modest vision in the early part of the century, exists as a significant political and social force in the 1980s; it has become a respectable ideology. The rise of a militant Israel defending itself against the Arab majority has excited the imaginations of Jewish youth and increased their interest in Judaism.

Some Jewish feminists and Marxists abandoned their connections with Judaism and devoted their energies to feminism in a way reminiscent of the ideology and life style of Rose Pastor Stokes and Emma Goldman. But they have had to confront the anti-Semitism and blatantly anti-Israel stance of many leftist groups. Where they choose to devote their energies remains an intensely personal decision; which force predominates—Judaism, feminism, Marxism, and/or Zionism—varies from rebel to rebel. Like-minded people cluster together to form groups, but one major organization encompassing all Jewish women rebels has not, and probably will not, emerge. It is very much within the Jewish and human culture to create multiple institutions and responses, and Jewish radicals are no exception to this tendency.

The generational perspective on the lives of Jewish American women offers two distinct possibilities: either each generation possesses all of the social types described in these pages, or there is change (for better or worse) from one generation to another. I think there is evidence for both points of view. The Bella Abzugs and Betty Friedans of the 1970s shared philosophical and cultural ties to the Rose Pastor Stokeses and Emma Goldmans of the 1890s generation. The authentic wish for social justice and women's rights motivated both generations of women. Alternately, the dramatic growth in the phenomenon of the Jewish woman professional since the 1960s has resulted in the displacement of much of the volunteer activists' work. This change in generational behavior has altered the nature of the Jewish woman's public participation.

Indeed, in the 1980s, there are multiple generations of Jewish women living side by side. As the Jewish population ages, with barely zero population growth to replace the adult generation, Jews find fewer younger people around them; yet, thanks to improved health standards, more older people are thriving. Jewish senior citizens have become both the clients and the volunteers for Jewish social services. They attend the lectures and cultural events provided by the Jewish community at the same time that they act as volunteer visitors to the sick and infirm. Three generations of Hadassah members sit side by side at the annual luncheon. In contrast to the immigrant generation's relationship to the German Jews already established in America, Jews in the 1980s all share a comfortable identification with this country.

It is to the credit of the Judaic culture, in contrast to the youth-oriented American culture, that Jewish Americans provide communal ties and services to older Jews. Jews remain members of their synagogues all of their lives; they attend Jewish community center activities; and they live in Jewish-sponsored senior citizens' homes. Will Jewish American women, especially the younger generation, continue to identify as Jews? Will they continue to be identified as Jewish volunteer activists, Jewish professionals, and Jewish writers? Or will their American identities blur all other associations? Is there a future for the Jewish woman volunteer in an increasingly professional world? Can the two distinctive aspects of the Jewish American woman's life be kept in active unity? Has the current generation achieved a natural dual identity? These are some of the questions that remain as the twentieth century draws to a close.

These questions are not uniquely mine. Jews are nothing if not keen observers of their own lives. Jewish writers have been scrutinizing and analyzing the present and the future of Jews in every time period and every place they have lived. Of the plethora of literature on the fate of the Jewish American community, however, only a small fragment deals specifically with Jewish American women. Jewish commentators, overwhelmingly male, rarely focus upon Jewish women. In the early 1970s, when the women's liberation movement became visible and vocal, Jewish commentators studied the connections between Judaism and feminism and tried to determine whether feminism was good for the Jews. The verdict was mixed, as would be expected; Orthodox rabbis decried the Jewish feminist critique of Judaism while some Reform and Conservative rabbis acknowledged the need for Judaism to adapt to feminist needs. Both the critics and sympathizers usually recognized the Jewish roots of the Jewish feminist claims. As Leo Pfeffer noted:

> As in the communist revolution, Jews have been prominent in the intellectual leadership of the feminist revolution—Marx, Trotsky and Rosa Luxemburg in the former, and Emma Goldman, Betty

Friedan and Shulamith Firestone in the latter.[7]

Although feminism may not portend well for traditional Judaism, it has been recognized that social criticism is a very Jewish enterprise and that Jewish women have been participating in that tradition alongside Jewish men.

Pfeffer's essay described the flexibility of rabbinic Judaism and the historic willingness of the Jewish community to evolve according to community dictates. He concluded:

> The feminist revolution is not an enemy of the Jewish people and should not be treated as such. It presents a challenge that can be met and lived with, else it will not for long survive as a living faith. It is difficult to live with change; it is impossible to live without it.[8]

In 1973, the Conservative Jewish synagogues declared a willingness to allow women to participate in the *minyan*, an important step toward full participation in the prayer service and one that Reform Judaism had long before granted women. In both Conservative and Reform prayer services, women had already been granted the right to open the ark of the Torah and to sit alongside the men. These fundamental changes in the worship ritual, traditionally an exclusively male domain, signaled profound change in Jewish practice.

Although the feminist movement, with its Jewish leadership, is influencing and slowly changing traditional Judaism, many of the Jewish feminists are inspired by feminism, not Judaism. Shulamith Firestone's *Dialectics of Sex* is an extreme, bitter analysis of Western society; traditional religion and capitalism both emerge as irretrievably evil forces that prevent women's liberation. While Phyllis Chesler sees important connections between her Judaism and her feminism, she identifies most strongly as a feminist, as does Betty Friedan. Judaism may offer the source of energy and perspective for feminism, but its influence is not central to some of the Jewish feminists. However, many Jewish feminists have affected thoughtful Jews who wish to combine the best of the new thought with the wisdom of the Jewish tradition.

Over 450 women attended the first National Conference of Jewish Women in February 1973 in New York City, a good sign of the interest in exploring and preserving the links between Judaism and feminism. As one reporter noted:

> What [the women] had in common was an overwhelming need to

find liberation in *Jewish* terms, in the Jewish community, with reference to Jewish men and Jewish children and Jewish values.[9]

The conference brought together Jewish women of diverse backgrounds to share their common concerns. Orthodox and Reform Jewish women, young and older women, mothers and daughters talked late into each night. Bluma Greenberg, a lecturer in Jewish studies, a rabbi's wife, and the mother of five children, argued that Jewish women "need not buy the whole package of women's liberation."[10] As an Orthodox Jew and one conscious of the destruction of six million Jews under Hitler, she argued that abortion was not a Jewish solution.

Rabbi Saul Berman, Chairman of the Department of Jewish Studies of Stern College for Women, one of the three men invited to speak at the conference, said that "By celebrating women, we have succeeded in winning their voluntary compliance in a role which puts them down."[11] Contrary to most Orthodox arguments that women's role in Judaism is a noble one, Rabbi Berman, a leader of the Orthodox Stern College for Jewish Women, challenged that position. The three-and-a-half-day conference succeeded in raising many women's awareness; that is, in making them rethink their role in Judaism. Many college-age participants and young women homemakers returned to their homes and formed support groups for Jewish women interested in working through their relationship with Judaism. Ezrat Nashim is the name of one such group formed in New York City. Others talked about communal living arrangements for like-minded people.

The public nature of this meeting, which was covered by the Jewish press although not effectively by the American press, suggests an exciting new debate on a subject in which women have rarely participated. Discussions of Jewish law have been within the male province since time immemorial; for the first time, Jewish women, with their new feminist perspective, are studying halachah, Jewish law, and debating the issues in very much the same way rabbinic students have done in seminaries throughout Jewish history. The very process of study and debate of, for example, traditional laws regarding marriage and divorce is likely to bring about change within the rabbinical courts. Predictably, Reform and Conservative Judaism will respond more swiftly than Orthodox Judaism, but many of the most sincere and serious critics of the tradition are Orthodox

Jewish women who want to preserve Judaism while making it recognize the dignity and equality of women. The feminist debate and struggle within Judaism will continue for a very long time. The patient feminist will doggedly work within the tradition while trying to change it; the impatient might seek liberal, experimental synagogues within which to worship.

One articulate and novel defender of the Orthodox view of women is Professor Lucy Davidowicz of Yeshiva University. In a brief piece entitled "Being a Woman in Shul" which appeared in *Commentary* magazine in 1968, Davidowicz contended that she is very comfortable sitting in a segregated section of the synagogue, apart from the men in the main section. She enjoyed the womanly gossip every Saturday morning and, more importantly, believed that the alternative, the equalization of women in the synagogue, would augur ill for Judaism. She envisioned one of two outcomes if women were treated equally in the synagogue: the "Italianization" or "Hadassahization" of the shul. In the former case, the model would be that of the Italian Catholic Church, with an adored priest and an all-female congregation while the men stayed away entirely. In Hadassahization, the synagogue would be transformed into a fundraising and cultural institution with prayer disappearing from its midst.[12]

Professor Davidowicz's theory is surely an interesting and unique one. Unfortunately, it shares the antifeminists bias of the Orthodox defenders of the status quo. This view assumes that women are not spiritual beings and are incapable of prayer and study. Their domain is the home and their place in the synagogue is ancillary at best. Religion, being a serious business, is the province of men, not women. Once women enter the male institution as equals, that institution is doomed. This argument does not speak well for the vitality of the institution or the ability of men to adapt to a new human situation. If prayer is an important human activity, it must be important for both sexes. Women have the intellectual and spiritual qualities required for prayer and study, and it is the very unwillingness of the Orthodox to recognize this fact that makes some Jewish women search for alternative religious experiences.

Although Davidowicz's viewpoint is novel, it remains within the traditional perspective. Once one departs from the established tradition, far more possibilities present themselves. How much custom should be preserved and how many rituals should be altered or abandoned? Who decides? Once the prospect of change is introduced, confusion along with reason and order enter the universe. Predictability falls before the new unpredictability. But the trend toward change in the rituals and practices of the synagogue is already under way. Girls of thirteen are now joining their brothers for the Bar Mitzvah ceremony; mothers are standing on the podium alongside their husbands for the first time; and special new prayers are being recited for the birth of a daughter.

Each Jewish woman who has had a successful public life has had to come to terms with her parents' and husband's attitudes toward Judaism as well as her own beliefs and ambitions. There is no uniform view of the "proper" relationship between ritual observance, cultural identity, and personal identity. Jewish men, of course, face the same dilemma. But, as suggested in numerous ways throughout this book, Jewish women who asserted themselves as individuals often acted against the Judaic tradition and the general American culture. Jewish women rebels and professionals, probably more so than women in any other type of public role described, deviated from both the Jewish and American cultures' views of women.

Jewish American women are both accurate barometers of the tensions and struggles within the Jewish American community as well as atypical examples of American womanhood. The ability of a Henrietta Szold, for example, to adapt to the dual role of a religiously observant woman performing a highly unusual and "unfemale" administrative role in a foreign country must strike the observer as extraordinary. The persistence of anarchist Emma Goldman in proclaiming her truths in spite of continued resistance is another example of atypical female behavior. The Jewish woman volunteer activist, on the other hand, has incorporated both the Jewish and American views of proper behavior for a woman. As a wife and mother who devotes some of her time to her community, she does not endanger the traditional sex-role definitions. The dual identity as a Jewish woman and an American is easily preserved.

But the new definition of identity for Jewish American women is harder to meld. It is an identity that must integrate a sense of selfhood, Judaism, and womanhood. Americans have always espoused the rhetoric of individual development, but only recently has the concept been applied to women. The Judeo-Christian tradition has emphasized the woman's role within the family. A Jewish woman is some man's daughter, wife, and mother. She never had a self separate from the family and communal context. Thus the philosophy of the feminist movement questions the traditional religious definition of Jewish womanhood.

Hillel said: "If I am not for myself, who is for me? And if I am only for myself, what am I? And not now, when?" This wise saying, quoted repeatedly in Jewish texts, has especial poignancy for contemporary Jewish women. The assertiveness of the women's movement has reminded Jewish women that they have a self worth knowing and developing. The middle statement points up the age-old Jewish commitment to the social fabric and the Jewish woman's obligation to care for her family and community. And it is the difficult task of Jewish American women to create a solution, however tentative and impermanent, that enables them to satisfy the multiple demands upon them.

The mergers to be developed do not have to conform to already expected images. Jewish American women do not have to abandon volunteer activities for professional careers; self-fulfillment does not necessarily mean paid employment. However, contrary to Cynthia Ozick's interpretation of the feminist movement, feminism is a powerful philosophy whose appeal cannot be underestimated. Jewish American women have been raised in an atmosphere that extols human achievement and individualism. Well-educated Jewish women want to express their will, intellect, and ambition. They want to perform and accomplish in the public sphere. They want personal satisfaction and society's rewards. But many also want to preserve the Jewish family, holiday celebrations, and the Jewish community. Jewish American women will continue to pursue personal, family, and social goals and in so doing will shape new forms for their public lives.

On the basis of the immediate past, one can only speculate as to future possibilities for Jewish American women. There appear to be emerging three social types with varying ties to the Jewish community. The first is the Orthodox Jewish woman, who will remain a distinct minority type but will persevere. She will continue to marry young, have a large family, and practice traditional Judaism. Although she will be better educated than her mother, and often practice a profession while rearing her family, she will continue to wear the traditional *shatel*, sit in a segregated portion of the synagogue, and go to the *mikvah* (ritual bathhouse) according to Jewish law. The second type will be a Jewish woman of the Conservative or Reform persuasion who will integrate her Judaism comfortably with all other aspects of her life. She may work as a professional, a part-time employee, or a volunteer in the community in Jewish or nonsectarian organizations. Although her Judaism will be an essential aspect of her identity, it may or may not be central to her existence; nor will she necessarily work only in Jewish institutions or causes.

The third type will be the cultural Jewish woman who will have little or no religious identification with Judaism; she will not belong to a synagogue or temple and her children will have no religious-school experience. She will consider herself a Jew but the term will have limited functional meaning. The cultural Jewish woman will be sympathetic to liberal social causes and intellectual pursuits; she may contribute to Israel and belong to Hadassah, but she will also belong to the League of Women Voters. The latter type, I suspect, will comprise the majority by the beginning of the twenty-first century. The powerful push toward absorption into the American culture is compelling. However, the first two types combined will continue to represent an active Jewish constituency, perhaps forty percent of Jewish American women. They will be sufficient in numbers to perpetuate a conscious Jewish identity and culture.

The cohesiveness of Judaism never could withstand the temptations of America. In order to succeed in this country, the Jew had to give up his separateness, his differentness, from the Protestant majority. The ghetto walls had to be breached and the influences of the outer world allowed inside. It is a testimony to Jewish Americans' adaptability and resiliency that they have been able to preserve something of their separateness while mingling with the Gentile world, but the essential, organic nature of Judaism has been lost in the blend, except for the minority who have remained zealously Orthodox. The observance of the Sabbath, of dietary laws, of the *mikvah*, and of all the religious holidays has not been possible for the majority of Jews in America. The total isolation of Jews has not been possible nor desired by most Jewish Americans.

In a sense, the seeds of organic dissolution are contained within Judaism itself. The universalist and particularist themes of the Judaic culture contain the basis for its merging with the larger culture. The moral truths of Judaism, the concern for social justice, and the humane values apply to all mankind. However, the beliefs in the Jews as the Chosen People, in the special relation of God to the Jews, and in the existence of Israel as the Promised Land lend a particularistic quality to Judaism, a quality that sets Jews apart from all others. The tension within American Judaism, however, consists in the question: How can Jewish Americans preserve their particularity while living in an American, a universalistic, environment? America encourages a blurring of religious distinctions and an emphasis upon the sameness of religions rather than the differences. In this environment, it is very difficult to preserve the distinctiveness of Judaism.

This important dilemma expresses itself through many of the social types we have discussed in this book. The Jewish woman writer, the Jewish social and volunteer worker, and the Jewish feminist-activist all have to deal with the question of whether their work and/or identity is particularly Jewish or universalistic. Cynthia Ozick argues that Jewish writers should write about Jewish themes and Jewish concerns, while other Jewish writers argue for the universality of their imaginative work. Jewish women volunteers in Jewish organizations have to ponder the Jewish content of their work when they discover that the recipients of their aid are Gentiles as well as Jews. Further, Jewish social-service agencies receive funds from nonsectarian sources such as the United Way and are therefore obligated to care for Gentiles. Can Jewish social-welfare institutions preserve their Jewish identity in the face of rising outside funding?

Jewish feminists must confront the issue of whether their primal identity is as feminists or as Jews—the universal versus the particular in another context. Or can they achieve a harmony of the two identities? How can the Jew remain particularly Jewish, and live and work in a Jewish atmosphere, while also connecting with Gentiles and secular concerns? Or can a Jewish woman whose daily life is lived in an un-Jewish world consider herself Jewish? Many of the women described in this book carved out a successful merger of both cultures. The nature and extent of that collaboration for future generations cannot be predicted.

Since Judaism has become a component and no longer the organic whole of a Jewish American's life, the balance of the Jewish and the secular ingredients is difficult to measure. If the trend toward professionalization continues, and work remains the major human endeavor of all adults, including female adults, how can people retain their religious-cultural identification? This question, of course, should concern all religious groups. But for Jewish women, especially those who gained a major source of gratification from volunteer social-welfare work, this question is very important. While Israel will remain a major uniting force for Jewish Americans for many years to come, the religious and communal ties of Jewish America will require a redefinition in order to persist.

The Jewish home, the synagogue, the Jewish women's organizations, and the Jewish social-service agencies all have played important roles in perpetuating active links to Judaism. They all are based upon the vital involvement of Jewish women. The first two projected types of Jewish women will carry on these links. But they will be faced, in their lives and their children's lives, with competing claims: the drive for self-fulfillment, the questioning of tradition by all Americans, and the antihistorical bias of contemporaries. Whether she knows it or not, the Jewish American woman, in all of her diversity, is a very important force for either positive change, drift, or the final abandonment of Judaism in America. Some twentieth-century Jewish American women have demonstrated, by their life's work, that a healthy harmony can be maintained between the best of both cultures. Their lives remain a model for this and future generations of Jewish American women.

Notes

2. JEWISH WOMEN WORKERS

1. Eighty-five percent of the production of men's clothing and ninety-five percent of women's clothing was produced by Jewish manufacturers.

2. Melech Epstein, *Jewish Labor in the U.S.A.*, 2 vols. in 1 (New York: Ktav, 1969), p. 388.

3. Louis Levine, *The Women's Garment Workers: A History of the International Ladies Garment Workers Union* (New York: B.W. Huebsch, 1924), p.154.

4. Levine, p. 156.

5. William Mailly, "The Working Girls' Strike," *Independent* 67 (December 23, 1909): 1419.

6. Epstein, p. 395.

7. Quoted in Abraham J. Karp, *Golden Door to America: The Jewish Immigrant Experience* (New York: Viking Press, 1976), p. 165.

8. Abraham Reisin, "Save Your Dimes," in *Pushcarts and Dreamers*, ed. and trans. Max Rosenfeld (New York: Thomas Yoseleff, 1967), p. 113.

9. Quoted in Karp, p. 155.

10. Quoted in Karp, p. 157.

11. Viola Paradise, "The Jewish Immigrant Girl in Chicago," *Survey* 30 (September 6, 1913): 703.

12. Levine, p. 431.

13. Quoted in Karp, p. 127.

14. Seymour Jacob Pomrenze, "Aspects of Chicago Russian-Jewish Life, 1893–1915," in *The Chicago Pinkas*, ed. Simon Rawidowicz (Chicago: College of Jewish Studies, 1952), p. 121.

15. Quoted in Karp, p. 150.

16. Melech Epstein, *The Jew and Communism: The Story of Early Communist Victories and Ultimate Defeats in the Jewish Community, U.S.A.. 1919#1941* (New York: Trade Union Sponsoring Committee, n.d.), p. xii.

17. Theresa Wolfson, "They Help Emancipate Womanhood," *American Hebrew* 122 (November 11, 1927): 21.

18. Quoted in Alice Kessler Harris, "Organizing the Unorganizable: Three Jewish Women and Their Union," *Labor History* 17 (Winter 1976): 13.

19. Quoted in a discussion about women voting in *Woman Citizen* 8 (March 22, 1924): 29–30.

20. Wolfson, p. 45.

21. Harris, pp. 5–23.

22. Quoted in Wolfson, p. 45.

23. Matthew Josephson, *Sidney Hillman: Statesman of American Labor* (New York: Doubleday, 1952).

24. Rudolf Glanz, *The Jewish Woman in America* (New York: Ktav, 1976), p. 84.

25. Ibid., p. 178, footnote 75.

26. Milton Doroshkin, *Yiddish in America: Social and Cultural Foundations* (Rutherford, N.J.: Fairleigh Dickinson University Press, 1969), pp. 144–146.

27. Ibid., p. 152.

28. Quoted in Doroshkin, p. 145.

29. Paradise, p. 703.

30. Ibid.

31. Elizabeth G. Stern, *My Mother and I* (New York: Macmillan, 1917), p. 48.

32. Mary Antin, *The Promised Land* (1912), p. 33, quoted in Allen Guttmann, *The Jewish Writer in America: Assimilation and the Crisis of Identity* (New York: Oxford University Press, 1971), p. 26.

33. Wise's *Reminiscences*, p. 212 quoted in Glanz, p. 185, footnote 40.

34. Mrs. Benjamin Davis, "Chicago," in *The Russian Jew in the United States*, ed. Charles S. Bernheimer (1915: reprint ed., New York: August M. Kelley, 1971), p. 177.

35. Glanz, p. 179, footnote 8.

36. Ibid., p. 186, footnote 59.

37. Quoted in Glanz, p. 179, footnote 13.

38. Glanz, p. 186, footnote 55.

39. Stern, p. 55.

40. Quoted in Glanz, p. 185, footnote 46.

41. Glanz, p. 171, footnote 39.

42. Paradise, p. 703.

3. Inspired By Judaism: Radical Jewish Women Activists

1. Marvin Bressler, "Selected Family Patterns in W. I. Thomas' Unfinished Study of *The Bintl Brief*," *American Sociological Review* 17 (October 1952): p. 567.

2. Rudolf Glanz, *The Jewish Woman in America* (New York: Ktav, 1976), p. 55.

3. Quoted in Glanz, p. 170, footnote 26.

4. Isa. I : 17.

5. Quoted in Glanz, p. 153, footnote 1.

6. Quoted in Glanz, p. 170, footnote 27.

7. Quoted in Glanz, p. 170, footnote 28.

8. A.H. Fromenson, "Amusements and Social Life: New York," in *The Rus-*

sian Jew in the United States, ed. Charles S. Bernheimer (1915; reprint ed., New York: August M. Kelley, 1971), p. 225.

9. Ibid., pp. 225–226.

10. Walter B. Rideout, "O Workers' Revolution. . .The True Messiah,' " in *Critical Studies in American Jewish History,* ed. Jacob R. Marcus 3 (New York: Ktav, 1971), pp. 178–179.

11. Quoted in Glanz, p. 93.

12. Robert D. Reynolds, Jr., "The Millionaire Socialists: J.G. Phelps Stokes and His Circle of Friends" (Ph.D. thesis, University of South Carolina, 1974),m pp. 97–98.

13. Rose Pastor Stokes, "I Belong to the Working Class! " (Unpublished ms., Yale University Archives), p. 2.

14. Quoted in Reynolds, p. 106.

15. Quoted in Glanz, p. 93.

16. Quoted in Reynolds, p. 105.

17. *New York Times,* October 19, 1925, pp. 1–2.

18. Richard Drinnon, *Mother Earth,* vol. 1 (New York: Greenwood Reprint Corporation, 1968), p. 2.

19. Alix Shulman. *To the Barricades: The Anarchist Life of Emma Goldman* (New York: Crowell, 1971), p. 1.

20. Emma Goldman, *Living My Life,* vol. 1 (1931; reprint ed., New York: Da Capo, 1970), p. 25.

21. Emma Goldman, "On the Road," *Mother Earth* 2 (May 1907): 131.

22. Emma Goldman, "Observations and Comments," *Mother Earth* 1 (November 1906): 7.

23. Translated from the Jewish of Liebin, "The Child's Question," *Mother Earth* 1 (February 1907): 55.

24. Ibid., p. 58.

25. Emma Goldman, "The Situation in America," *Mother Earth* 2 (October 1907): 325.

26. Emma Goldman, "Observations and Comments," *Mother Earth* 3 (September 1908): 276–277.

27. Emma Goldman, "Defying the Gods," *Mother Earth* 3 (July 1908): 223.

28. Emma Goldman, "Adventures in the Desert of American Liberty," *Mother Earth* 4 (September 1909): 212.

29. Emma Goldman, "On the Trail," *Mother Earth* 5 (February 1911): 387.

30. Emma Goldman, "The Power of the Ideal," *Mother Earth* 7 (April 1912): 51–52.

31. Ibid., p. 53.

32. Emma Goldman, "Light and Shadows in the Life of an Avant-Guard," *Mother Earth* 5 (April 1910): 49.

33. Emma Goldman, "At Twenty-Six," *Mother Earth* 3 (October 1908): 332.

34. Quoted in Shulman, pp. 159–160.

35. Emma Goldman, *Anarchism and Other Essays,* 3rd rev. ed. (New York: Mother Earth, 1917), p. 217.

36. Melech Epstein, *The Jew and Communism: The Story of Early Communist Victories and Ultimate Defeats in the Jewish Community U.S.A. 1919#1941* (New York: Trade Union Sponsoring Committee, n.d.), pp. 3–5.

37. Ibid., p. 5.

38. Ibid., p. 23.

39. Ibid., p. 121.

40. Ibid., p. 203.

4. VOLUNTEER ACTIVISTS: THE FIRST TWO GENERATIONS

1. Henry Feingold, *Zion in America* (New York: Hippocrene Books, 1974) p. 125.

2. "The Week in Review," *American Hebrew* 122 (November 18, 1927): 19.

3. Max Vorspan and Lloyd P. Gartner, *History of the Jews of Los Angeles* (San Marino, Calif.: The Huntington Library, 1970), p. 139.

4. Joseph L. Blau, *Judaism in America: From Curiosity to Third Faith* (Chicago: University of Chicago Press, 1976), p. 133.

5. Lee K. Frankel, "Philanthropy: New York," in *The Russian Jew in the United States*, ed. Charles S. Bernheimer (1915: reprint ed., New York: August M. Kelley, 1971) pp. 62–99.

6. Vorspan and Gartner, p. 146.

7. Feingold, p. 209.

8. Philip P. Bregstone, *Chicago and Its Jews* (privately published, 1933), p. 45.

9. Ibid., p. 43.

10. Ibid.

11. Hannah G. Solomon, *Fabric of My Life* (New York: Bloch, 1946). p. 46.

12. Ibid., p. 81.

13. Quoted in Solomon, p. 87.

14. Quoted in Solomon, p. 90.

15. Solomon, p. 94.

16. Bernheimer, p. 348.

17. Solomon, p. 95.

18. Ibid., p. 107.

19. Ibid., p. 99.

20. Ibid., p. 106.

21. Rudolf Glanz, *The Jewish Woman in America* (New York: Ktav, 1976), pp. 164–165.

22. Rebekah Kohut, *As I Know Them: Some Jews and a Few Gentiles* (New York: Doubleday, Doran & Co., 1929), p. 119.

23. Ibid., p. 254.

24. Ibid., p. 257.

25. Rosa Sonneschein, "Notes," *The American Jewess* 2 (November 1895): 112.

26. Rosa Sonneschein, "The National Council of Jewish Women and our Dream of Nationality," *The American Jewess* 4 (October 1896): 29.

27. Ibid., p. 30.

28. Ibid., p. 32.

29. Solomon, p. 115.

30. Ibid., p. 200.

31. Rosa Sonneschein, "Editor's Desk," *The American Jewess* 2 (October 1895): 63.

32. Rosa Sonneschein, "Editor's Desk," *The American Jewess* 5 (May 1897): 97.

33. Rosa Sonneschein, "The Zionist Congress," *The American Jewess* 6 (October 1897): 20.

34. Mrs. Fels appeared on the masthead of *The Public* on August 10, 1917, and made her last appearance on March 8, 1919. In 1919, *The Public* merged with *The New Republic*.

35. Mary Fels, "Rebuilding Palestine," *The Public* 21 (January 4, 1918): 9.

36. Ibid., p. 10.

37. Marvin Lowenthal, *Henrietta Szold: Life and Letters* (New York: Viking Press, 1942) pp. 46–47.

38. Ibid., p. 53.

39. Quoted in Lowenthal, p. 86.

40. See Melvin Urofsky, *American Zionism from Herzl to the Holocaust* (New York: Anchor Press, 1975) pp. 140–144.

41. Joan Dash, *Summoned to Jerusalem* (New York: Harper & Row, 1979), p. 203.

42. Quoted in Yonathan Shapiro, *Leadership of the American Zionist Organization 1897–1930* (Urbana: University of Illinois Press, 1971), p. 204.

43. Dash, p. 202.

44. Quoted in Lowenthal, p. 51.

45. Quoted in Lowenthal, p. 183.

46. Quoted in Lowenthal, p. 261.

47. Alexandra Lee Levin, *The Szolds of Lombard Street: A Baltimore Family 1859–1909* (Philadelphia: JPS of America, 1960) p. 202.

48. Nelson G. Kraschel, "Iowa: Jews Benefit Philanthropy," *The American Hebrew* 142 (December 10, 1937): p. 40.

49. Frieda Mogerman, "Pioneers in Social Service: The Jewish Committee for Personal Service in State Institutions in the 1920s," *Western States Jewish Historical Quarterly* 41 (January 1974): 83.

50. Ibid.

51. "Sisterhood Number," *The American Hebrew* 122 (January 6, 1928): 309.

52. Quoted in "Sisterhood Number," p. 315.

53. Paula Pfeffer, "Portrait of a Reformer: Esther Loeb Kohn" (Master's thesis, Northeastern Illinois University, 1974).

54. Pfeffer utilized the Esther Loeb Kohn papers at the University of Illinois at Chicago Circle in her research.

55. Quoted in Pfeffer, p. 27.

56. Pfeffer, p. 21.

57. Ibid., p. 33.

58. "Notes," *The American Hebrew* 142 (November 26, 1937): 12.

5. VOLUNTEER ACTIVISTS: 1945–1980

1. Doris B. Gold, "Beyond the Valley of the Shmattes: A Meditation on Jewish Women's Organizations," *Lilith* 1 (Fall 1976): 30.

2. Fred Massarik, *National Jewish Population Study* (New York: Council of Jewish Federations and Welfare Funds, n.), p. 2. Massarik states that forty-four percent of all Jewish households were members of a congregation in 1970.

3. Ibid., p. 1.

4. Conference of Jewish Women's Organizations, *Official Directory, 1950–1951* (Chicago: Conference of Jewish Women's Organizations, 1950).

5. Claire M. Aronson, "Women," reprinted in *Chicago Sentinel* (August 1948), special issue, *100 Years of Chicago Jewry*, p. 3.

6. Steven M. Cohen, Susan Dessel, and Michael Pelavin, "Women's Power and Status in Jewish Communal Life: A Look at the UJA," *Response* 9 (Winter 1975–1976): 59–66.

7. Amy Stone, "The Locked Cabinet," *Lilith* (Winter 1976–1977): 19–20.

8. Gold, p. 32.

9. Elsa Solender, "Where Are the Women?" *Moment* 2 (June 1977): 63.

10. Cohen, Dessel, and Pelavin, pp. 59–66.

11. Stone, pp. 17–20.

12. Jacqueline Levine, "The Changing Role of Women in the Jewish Community," *Response* 6 (Summer 1973): 61.

13. Solender, pp. 34–36.

14. Cynthia Fuchs Epstein, "Mind, Matter and Mentors: The Making of a Sociologist," in *The Frontiers of Knowledge*, ed. Judith Stiehm (Los Angeles: University of Southern California Press, 1976), p. 26.

15. Gold, p. 31.

6. JEWISH WOMEN WRITERS

1. Robert Alter, *After the Tradition* (New York: E.P. Dutton, 1971), p. 38.

2. Cynthia Ozick, "The Evasive Jewish Story," *Midstream* 12 (February 1966): 79.

3. Muriel Rukeyser, "To Be a Jew in the Twentieth Century," in *The Literature of American Jews*, ed. Theodore L. Gross (New York: Free Press, 1973), p. 338.

4. Fannie Hurst, *Song of Life* (New York: Alfred A. Knopf, 1927), p. 63.

5. Ibid., p. 71.

6. Ibid., p. 96.
7. Ibid., p. 73.
8. Ibid., pp. 73–73.
9. Anzia Yezierska, *Bread Givers* (1925; reprint ed., New York: George Braziller, 1975), p. 284.
10. Anzia Yezierska, "Hunger," in *A Treasury of American Jewish Stories*, ed. Harold U. Ribalow (New York: Thomas Yoseloff, 1958), p. 336.
11. Hortense Calisher, *The Collected Stories of Hortense Calisher* (New York: Arbor House, 1975), pp. 224–245.
12. Ibid., p. 264.
13. Ibid., p. 273.
14. Grace Paley, *Enormous Changes at the Last Minute* (New York: Dell, 1975), p. 41.
15. Ibid., p. 86.
16. Ibid., pp. 204–205.
17. Ibid., p. 95.
18. Ibid.
19. Ibid., p. 40.
20. Tillie Olsen, *Tell Me a Riddle* (New York: Dell, 1976), p. 75.
21. Ibid., p. 89.
22. Ibid., p. 90.
23. Ibid., p. 125.
24. Gail Parent, *Sheila Levine Is Dead and Living in New York* (New York: Bantam Books, 1972), p. 3.
25. Ibid., pp. 171–172.
26. Norma Rosen, *Green: A Novella and Eight Stories* (New York: Harcourt, Brace & World, 1967), p. 97.
27. Edna Ferber, *Fanny Herself* (1917; reprint ed., New York: Arno Press, 1975), p. 4.
28. Ibid., p. 11.
29. Ibid.
30. Ibid., p. 37.
31. Edna Ferber, *A Kind of Magic* (New York: Doubleday, 1963), p. 286.
32. Edna Ferber, *A Peculiar Treasure* (Garden City, New York: Doubleday, Doran & Co., 1939), p. 165.
33. Ferber, *Magic*, p. 124.
34. Fannie Hurst, *Anatomy of Me* (New York: Doubelday, 1958) p. 105.
35. Ibid., p. 188.
36. Anzia Yezierska, *Red Ribbon on a White Horse* (New York: Charles Scribner's Sons, 1950), p. 97.
37. Cynthia Ozick, *The Pagan Rabbi and Other Stories* (New York: Alfred A. Knopf, 1971), p. 177.
38. Cynthia Ozick, "Bloodshed," *Esquire* 85 (January 1976): 138.
39. Cynthia Ozick, "Usurpation," *Esquire* 81 (May 1974): 126.
40. Cynthia Ozick, "Living in Two Cultures," *Response* 6 (Fall 1972): 87–93.

41. Cynthia Ozick, "America: Toward Yavheh," *Judaism* 19 (Summer 1970): 275.

42. Cynthia Ozick, "All the World Wants the Jews Dead," *Esquire* 82 (November 1974): 207.

43. Cynthia Ozick, "A Liberal's Auschwitz," in *The Pushcart Prize: Best of the Small Presses*, ed. Bill Henderson (New York: Avon Books, 1976), p. 150.

44. Ibid., p. 153.

45. Ibid., p. 152.

46. Cynthia Ozick, "All the World," p. 208.

47. Ozick, "America," p. 276.

48. Ibid.

49. Cynthia Ozick, "Notes Toward Finding the Right Question," *Lilith* 6 (1979): 19–29.

50. Ibid., p. 25.

7. SUCCESSFUL MERGERS

1. David S. Lifson, *The Yiddish Theater in America* (New York: Thomas Yoseloff, 1965), p. 177.

2. Ronald Sanders, *The Downtown Jews* (New York: New American Library, 1976), p. 257.

3. Quoted in A. H. Fromenson, "New York: Amusements and Social Life," in *The Russian Jews in the United States*, ed. Charles S. Bernheimer (1915; reprint ed., New York: August M. Kelley, 1971), p. 229.

4. Quoted in Lifson, p. 163.

5. Quoted in Rudolf Glanz, *The Jewish Woman in America* (New York: Ktav, 1976), p. 157.

6. Lifson, p. 157.

7. Personal interview with Dina Halpern, May 2, 1977.

8. Biographical details of Sophie Tucker's life were taken from Sophie Tucker, *Some of These Days: The Autobiography of Sophie Tucker* (Garden City, New York: Garden City Publishing Co., 1945).

9. Quoted in John E. Dimeglio, *Vaudeville U.S.A.* (Bowling Green, Ohio: Bowling Green University Popular Press, 1973), p. 60.

10. Told in Katharine Roberts, "Your Gal Sophie," *Collier's* (February 19, 1938): 29.

11. Norman Katkov, *The Fabulous Fanny: The Story of Fanny Brice* (New York: Alfred A. Knopf, 1953).

12. Ibid., p. 205.

13. Ruth Sapinsky, "The Jewish Girl at College," *Menorah Journal* 2 (December 1916): 297–298.

14. Ruth Sapin Hurwitz, "Coming of Age at Wellesley," *Menorah Journal* 38 (Autumn 1950): 232.

15. Sidney Goldstein, "American Jewry: A Demographic Analysis," in *The Future of the American Jewish Community in America*, ed., David Sidorsky (New York: Basic Books, 1973), p. 109.

16. Alvin Chenkin, "Demographic Highlights," in *National Jewish Population Study* (New York: Council of Jewish Federations and Welfare Funds, 1976), p. 22.

17. "Years of School Completed by Americans," *The Chronicle of Higher Education* (September 13, 1976): 12.

18. Selma C. Berrol, "Superintendent Julia Richman: A Social Progressive in the Public Schools," *Elementary School Journal* 72 (May 1972): 402–411.

19. Quoted in Berrol, p. 404.

20. Selma Berrol, "When Uptown Met Downtown: Julia Richman's Work in the Jewish Community of New York, 1880–1912," *American Jewish History* 70 (September, 1980): 35–51.

21. Ibid., p. 42.

22. Quoted in Berrol, p. 45.

23. Quoted in "A Friend of East-Side Children," *The Literary Digest* 45 (July 13, 1912): 65.

24. Quoted in Sara Feinstein, "Opening Opportunities for Women in Jewish Communal Service," *Journal of Jewish Communal Service* 52 (Winter 1975): 159.

25. Feinstein, pp. 153–162.

26. "Notes," *The American Hebrew* 142 (January 14, 1938): 13.

27. Morris Fine and Milton Himmelfarb, eds. *American Jewish Yearbook* 74 (New York: American Jewish Committee, 1973): 566.

28. Carl Urbont, "The Avowed and Operating Purposes of the Contemporary Jewish Community Center Movement" (Ed.D. thesis, Columbia University, 1966), p. 24.

29. William Chafe, *The American Woman* (New York: Oxford University Press, 1972), p. 91.

30. Feinstein, pp. 153–162.

31. Ibid., p. 158.

32. This information is based upon numerous accounts reported in the *New York Times*.

33. *New York Times*, October 19, 1934, p. 25.

34. Zelda Popkin, "Sociological Court is Urged for Women" *New York Times*, November 25, 1934, 8, p. 5.

35. *New York Times*, July 15, 1964, p. 34.

36. Marcia R. Rudin, "Women Rabbis," *Present Tense* 6 (Winter 1979): 48.

37. Rabbi Samuel K. Joseph, National Director of Admissions and Alumni Affairs, Hebrew Union College-Jewish Institute of Religion, personal communication, May 28, 1980.

38. Rudin, p. 44.

39. David M. Szonyi, "The Book Reporter," *Women's American ORT Reporter* (March/April 1977): 6.

40. David Szonyi, "The Conservative Condition," *Moment* 5 (May 1980): 38.

41. *Chicago Sun-Times*, May 24, 1980, p. 21.

42. "Our Readers Speak: Women as Rabbis," *Moment* 5 (May 1980): 34–37.

43. Gladys Rosen, "Can the Women's Movement Save the Jewish Family?" *Jewish Digest* 24 (July/August 1979): 14.

44. Joseph, personal communication.

45. Aviva Cantor Zuckoff, "An Exclusive Interview with Dr. Phyllis Chesler," *Lilith* (Winter 1976/1977): 24.

46. Ibid., p. 29.

47. Cynthia Fuchs Epstein, "Mind, Matter, and Mentors: The Making of a Sociologist," in *The Frontiers of Knowledge*, ed. Judith Stiehm (Los Angeles, University of Southern California Press, 1976), pp. 23–24.

8. FUTURE DIRECTIONS

1. Vivian Jacobson, Expansion Chairwoman for Chicago Hadassah, reports a dramatic increase in membership and interest among younger women in the year 1979–1980.

2. Nathan Glazer, "The New Left and the Jews," in *The Jewish Community in America*, ed. Marshall Sklare (New York: Behrman House, 1974), p. 306.

3. Jack Nusen Porter and Peter Dreier, eds., *Jewish Radicalism: A Selected Anthology* (New York: Grove Press, 1973), p. xxi.

4. Ibid.

5. Judith Plaskow, "The Jewish Feminist: Conflict in Identities," in Elizabeth Koltun, ed., *The Jewish Woman: New Perspectives* (New York: Schocken, 1976), p. 3.

6. Nechama Liss-Levinson sent the blessing in to the "Letters" column of *Ms.* magazine, March 1974, p. 7.

7. Leo Pfeffer, "Feminism and Judaism," *Congress Monthly* 42 (June 1975): 12.

8. Ibid., p. 14.

9. Susan Dworkin, "Women of Valor," *Hadassah Magazine* 54 (April 1973): 14.

10. Quoted in Dworkin, p. 15.

11. Quoted in Dworkin, p. 37.

12. Lucy Davidowicz, "On Being a Woman in Shul," *Commentary* 46 (July 1968): 71–74.

Selected Bibliography

Charlotte Baum, Paula Hyman, and Sonya Michel, *The Jewish Woman in America* (New York: Dial Press, 1976).

Philip Cowen, *Memories of an American Jew* (New York: International Press, 1932).

Joan Dash, *Summoned to Jerusalem: The Life of Henrietta Szold* (New York: Harper & Row, 1979).

Cathy N. Davidson and E.M. Broner, eds., *The Lost Tradition: Mothers and Daughters in Literature* (New York: Frederick Ungar, 1980).

Milton Doroshkin, *Yiddish in America: Social and Cultural Foundations* (Rutherford, N.J.: Farleigh Dickinson University Press, 1969).

Melech Epstein, *Jewish Labor in the U.S.A.: Industrial, Political, and Cultural History of the Jewish Labor Movement, 1882–1914* (New York: Ktav, 1969).

———, *The Jew and Communism: The Story of Early Communist Victories and Ultimate Defeats in the Jewish Community, U.S.A., 1919-1941* (New York: Trade Union Sponsoring Committee, n.d.).

Henry L. Feingold, *Zion in America: The Jewish Experience from Colonial Times to the Present* (New York: Twayne, 1974).

Rudolph Glanz, *The Jewish Woman In America: The Eastern European Jewish Woman* (New York: Ktav, 1976).

Milton M. Gordon, *Assimilation in American Life: The Role of Race, Religion, and National Origins* (New York: Oxford University Press, 1964).

Irving Howe, *World of Our Fathers* (New York: Harcourt Brace Jovanovich, 1976).

Samuel Joseph, *Jewish Immigration to the United States: From 1881 to 1910* (New York: Arno Press, 1969).

Rebekah Kohut, *As I Know Them: Some Jews and a Few Gentiles* (New York: Doubleday, Doran & Co., 1929).

Elizabeth Koltun, ed., *The Jewish Woman: New Perspectives* (New York: Schocken, 1976).

Lucy Robins Lang, *Tomorrow Is Beautiful* (New York: Macmillan, 1948).

Alexandra Lee Levin, *The Szolds of Lombard Street: A Baltimore Family, 1859–1909* (Philadelphia: Jewish Publication Society of America, 1960).

Marlin Levin, *Balm in Gilead: The Story of Hadassah* (New York: Schocken, 1973).

Louis Levine, *The Women Garment Workers: A History of the International Ladies Garment Workers Union* (New York: B.W. Huebsch, 1924).

Arthur Liebman, *Jews and the Left* (New York: Wiley, 1979).

Marvin Lowenthal, *Henrietta Szold: Life and Letters* (New York: Viking Press, 1942).

Andre Manners, *Poor Cousins* (New York: Coward, McCann & Georghegan, 1972).

Jack Nusan Porter and Peter Dreier, eds., *Jewish Radicalism: A Selected Anthology* (New York: Grove Press, 1973).

Moses Rischin, *The Promised City: New York's Jews, 1870–1914* (New York: Harper Torchbooks, 1970).

Alix Kates Shulman, *To the Barricades: The Anarchist Life of Emma Goldman* (New York: Thomas Y. Cromwell, 1971).

David Sidorsky, *The Future of the American Jewish Community in America* (New York: Basic Books, 1973).

Marshall Sklare, *The Jewish Community in America* (New York: Behrman House, 1974).

Barbara Miller Solomon, *Pioneers in Service: The History of the Associated Jewish Philanthropies of Boston* (Boston: Associated Jewish Philanthropies, 1956).

Rose Pastor Stokes, *The Woman Who Wouldn't* (New York: G.P. Putnam's Sons, 1916).

Goldie Stone, *My Caravan of Years: An Autobiography* (New York: Bloch, 1945).

Melvin Urofsky, *American Zionism from Herzl to the Holocaust* (New York: Anchor Press, 1975).

James Weinstein, *The Decline of Socialism in America* (New York: Vintage Books, 1969).

Index